Education and Care for Adolescents and Adults with Autism

Education and Care for Adolescents and Adults with Autism

Kate Wall

SAGE Publications
Los Angeles · London · New Delhi · Singapore

SAGE Publications Ltd
1 Oliver's Yard
55 City Road
London EC1Y 1SP

SAGE Publications Inc
2455 Teller Road
Thousand Oaks, California 91320

SAGE Publications India Pvt Ltd
B 1/I 1 Mohan Cooperative Industrial Area
Mathura Road
New Delhi 110 044

SAGE Publications Asia-Pacific Pte Ltd
33 Pekin Street #02–01
Far East Square
Singapore 048763

Library of Congress Control Number: 2007931827

A catalogue record for this book is available from the British Library

ISBN-978-1-4129-2381-1
ISBN-978-1-4129-2382-8 (pbk)

Typeset by Pantek Arts Ltd, Maidstone, Kent
Printed in Great Britain by TJ International, Padstow
Printed on paper from sustainable resources

Contents

Acknowledgements

My thanks go to Estelle, my friend and colleague, who has always encouraged and supported me in my writing, and has spurred me on when the going has been tough! Similar thanks must go to Jude Bowen, from Paul Chapman Publishing, for her ongoing support and belief in me.

No book can pass without acknowledgement of the unquestioning belief Sam and Tracy have in me, as both a mother and author. You both continue to be my inspiration and help me to maintain my own belief in myself at times. Without Michael my books simply would not happen and for this I owe him so much and somehow 'thanks' simply does not seem adequate enough.

This book is dedicated to Mum, as always, who always said I would write a book one day! How come she was usually right?

Glossary of Terms

AS	Asperger syndrome
ASD	autistic spectrum disorder
CSCI	Commission for Social Care Inspectorate
DES	Department of Education and Science
DfES	Department for Education and Skills
DHSS	Department of Health and Social Security
DLT	Daily Life Therapy
DoH	Department of Health
DRC	Disability Rights Commission
DWP	Department for Work and Pensions
ECM	Every Child Matters
EP	educational psychologist
FE	further education
GP	general practitioners
GSCC	General Social Care Council
HE	higher education
ICD-10	International Classification of Diseases (version 10)
IEP	individual education plan
KS1/2/3/4	Key Stage 1/2/3/4
LDAF	Learning Disability Awards Framework
LDTF	Learning Disability Task Force
LEA	local education authority
NAS	National Autistic Society
NASEN	National Association of Special Educational Needs
NCSC	National Care Standards Commission
NfER	National Foundation for Educational Research
NHS	National Health Service
NPSA	National Patient Safety Agency
NSF	National Service Framework
NVQ	National Vocational Qualifications
Ofsted	Office for Standards in Education
PCP	person-centred planning

PCT	Primary Care Trusts
PDD	pervasive developmental disorder
PDD-NOS	Pervasive developmental disorder – not otherwise specified
PECS	Picture Exchange Communication System
PSHE	personal, social and health education
QCA	Qualifications and Curriculum Authority
RBA	Removing Barriers to Achievement
SEBD	Social, emotional or behavioural difficulties
SEN	special educational needs
SENCO	special educational needs coordinator
SENDA	Special Educational Needs and Disability Discrimination Act
SSI	Social Services Inspectorate
TEACCH	Treatment and Education of Autistic and Related Communication Handicapped Children
WHO	World Health Organisation

About the Author

Kate Wall has over 20 years of experience of working with children and adults with special needs in both mainstream and special provision. She is a successful author with books such as *Special Needs and Early Years* (now in its second edition) and *Autism and Early Years Practice* to her name.

Early in her career, Kate found her place in provision for children with special needs, and became heavily involved in supporting the families of those children. This resulted in her determination to address the needs of each family member and not only the individual with special needs, as each has a significant impact on the other. During these years Kate also spent time working with adults with learning disabilities and developed a specific interest in autistic spectrum disorders (ASDs), which culminated in her current passion for improving the lives of those with ASDs and their family members.

In her current position as a Principal Lecturer at Canterbury Christ Church University, Kate has a responsibility to provide for all students with disabilities on her programme. Throughout her career she has always worked with professionals from other agencies and this is now a key focus in many of the current government strategies such as Every Child Matters, Youth Matters and Better Services for Adults with ASDs.

As well as writing books, she also writes magazine articles, delivers training and is a regular conference presenter.

1

Introduction to this book

This chapter will:
- ➤ introduce the reader to some of the key issues explored throughout this book;
- ➤ identify to the reader the topics covered within each chapter.

Throughout this book the world of autism and key characteristics for young people and adults with ASDs will be explored, considering the impact these will have on the health, education and care of those experiencing ASDs. The effect on family members will be discussed to raise awareness and understanding of the considerable impact that ASDs can have. Legislation and government initiatives will also be explored to highlight progress and developments to date. Specifically, reports related to provision for adolescents and adults with ASDs have emerged which will have helped develop our understanding of the key issues related to this particularly vulnerable group within our society. Such reports show that the current situation is clearly not addressing needs appropriately.

Throughout the development of the chapters you should realise that the information covered barely touches the surface and each chapter could itself have developed into another book. It is for this reason that I refer readers to additional, relevant reading at the end of each chapter. The bibliography containing books, journal articles, reports, guidance documents and websites should also provide additional sources of information for interested parties.

Many professionals are already engaged in positive and meaningful provision for those adolescents and adults they work with and hopefully this book will help confirm their positive contribution to work in this field. It is also hoped that the book may further enhance practice. For those professionals working with adolescents and adults with ASDs but lacking ASD-specific knowledge it is hoped that improved practice may result from engaging with this text. The people we are working with have a right to effective and appropriate practice, responding directly to their individual needs, and it is our responsibility to take this challenge and succeed. Whatever professional role we hold, we should identify any potential barriers and work to overcome them. The philosophy of *Valuing People* (DoH, 2001b) should be our philosophy, to enable rights, choice, inclusion and independence.

Chapter 2 considers some definitions and characteristics of ASDs along with an overview of current provision across health, education and social care. This provides the background information needed to explore subsequent chapters so professionals and carers can be well placed to understand ASDs in context. Without this knowledge it could be suggested that we cannot respond positively to the needs of the adolescents and adults we work with or care for. It will be seen that *for adolescents and adults with ASDs life can be complex and confusing*, so we should ensure we have the knowledge and skills required to reduce or eliminate as much complexity and confusion as possible to enable each individual to reach their full potential. This can be developed through education, transition plans, care plans, person-centred planning and advocacy services which identify every opportunity for further personal development to make life more fulfilling for the individual.

It will also come to light that *we need to focus on individual needs as opposed to categories of need* as no two adolescents or adults with ASD will present with the same difficulties. We need to explore the individual's current likes and dislikes, strengths and weaknesses alongside which areas we could work on in the future. All aspects of this information will help us to decide the most helpful strategies to adopt which are likely to bring about success. Sadly current legislation and guidance continues to categorise or segregate, as we see documentation for the majority and then separate documentation for those with special needs, learning disabilities and/or ASDs. If the government drive is for increased social and educational inclusion then the message coming from the government should be exactly that. *Good practice in education or health and social care for those with any learning difficulty is simply good practice – it is not a separate or discrete practice for a minority group*. In addition, *all documentation, whether it be legislation, a guidance document or a report, should utilise the same terminology to reduce confusion*. If we are moving to increased joint working, multidisciplinary practice or inter-agency working then so be it, but documentation should avoid confusion and ensure greater clarity.

Issues of diagnosis and labelling are highlighted, together with the fact that *there are likely to be many adults in adult provision without a diagnosis but who demonstrate ASD behaviours*. Due to the more recent increased availability of diagnoses in childhood this should be less of a problem in the future but for now we have many undiagnosed adults in our services. Further they may be placed in inappropriate settings which compound their needs further. This clearly needs addressing.

Discussion of the 'triad of impairments' will see the beginnings of our understanding of ASDs with the key areas of difficulty being identified as: social communication, social interaction and imagination. Difficulties in each of these areas should be present to secure a diagnosis and the NAS Screening for Adults could be accessed (Internet 1) and utilised if there is any doubt or to indicate the likelihood of an ASD. However, it should be remembered that only those professionals who are suitably qualified and experienced are able to offer a firm diagnosis. The reality for many adults with ASDs can be far from what we would wish for and the *Ignored or Ineligible* report (Barnard et al., 2001) highlights this very clearly. This should spur us on all the more to work to get it right whatever challenges and barriers are placed before us. *Arguably the most powerful tool we have will be our knowledge and understanding of ASDs, the impact they have and how to identify achievable and realistic goals for the future.*

Explorations of the current situation in both education and care provision will follow, identifying the current educational system for supporting adolescents with special educational needs, transition arrangements and then adult services provision. What has emerged is a vast diversity of provision in a range of settings, some of which have trained and highly qualified staff and others which do not. Additionally, the systems and processes in each setting do not always lend themselves to supporting those with ASDs effectively. All the guidance and reports suggest that adolescents and adults with disabilities (including ASDs) should receive high-quality provision based on assessed needs (DoH, 2001b). However, if not all young people are receiving meaningful transition plans (NAS, 2004) formulated in a person-centred planning philosophy with opportunities for advocacy, then how can the provision that follows be of high quality and meet individual needs? *Key areas of concern for adults with ASDs emerge as equality of access to: housing, education, employment, health care and leisure*, but again knowledge and understanding of ASDs by all professionals still remains fundamental to effective practice and support. Thus *training for all professionals involved in health, education and/or care is essential if we aim to respond more appropriately in the future.*

Chapter 3 focuses on policy, legislation and guidance relating to provision for adolescents and adults with ASDs from back in the days before autism was recognised as a specific disorder, when people demonstrating such behaviours would have been considered a danger to society and institutionalised, to the current day. The chapter is detailed – and I make no apologies for this – to place our current understanding firmly within a historical context. Understanding how we have arrived at the present position may help to develop our current understanding and possibly suggest where we may be heading in the future.

As the documentation spans education, health and social care it soon became clear that the amount of information that has emerged since the late 1990s is tremendous. However, this raises another key issue: *How can professionals be expected to remain up to date if there is so much information to access, read and interpret effectively?* In addition, *if agencies are expected to work more closely together in a 'seamless' manner then why do we still see documentation emerging from the different agencies? Does this not suggest a contradiction?* Hopefully readers will feel more positively informed about current initiatives and campaigns from national organisations fighting the case for adolescents and adults with ASDs, and the timeline at the end of the chapter should help to clarify understanding. *National policies, however, need clearer direction relating to ASDs to ensure ongoing and consistent improvements in provision.*

Chapter 4 focuses on the world of autism to offer readers a greater understanding of the areas of difficulty experienced by those with ASDs. Hopefully this knowledge will lead to improved practice as lack of knowledge can seriously compound the difficulties of those with ASDs. Again, knowledge and understanding is seen as of paramount importance. It is only with this knowledge that professionals can understand the needs of people with ASDs as the behaviours they may demonstrate are very individual but with some commonalities, and as such can be difficult to interpret accurately and manage. The specific, and classic, characteristics of ASDs are highlighted in some detail and case studies are offered to link the theoretical discussions to the realities of everyday life. The word 'play' in the context of this chapter refers to any leisure-type activities, e.g. playing cards or Scrabble, going for a drink with friends or a trip to the cinema.

A particular focus is placed on understanding and becoming more aware of sensory difficulties which may occur for some adolescents and adults with ASDs. Natural responses from professionals may involve physical touch and contact which can be physically painful. Other sensory issues to be explored are taste, smell, vision and hearing, each of which can have a significant impact on those affected. So again we see the importance of *issues of training, plus the funding to provide it.* If we are expecting all professionals across all agencies to become more knowledgeable in issues relating to ASDs then this should be established at a national level to ensure they have equal access to appropriate training. If this does not occur then it could be suggested that adolescents and adults with ASDs cannot experience appropriate provision. *We cannot continue to expect staff to instinctively possess or gain this crucial knowledge but must, in a coherent manner, ensure they are trained.*

A significant issue when working with adults with ASDs is that for some, who have competent and fluent verbal skills, the underlying lack of skills in other areas can easily be overlooked. This is due to assumptions being made by the listener. Adults with ASDs have reported consistently over the years that while they may be competent communicators on the outside, they cannot make themselves breakfast or go shopping and ensure they return with the correct items. Professionals should appreciate this and remain open-minded, never assuming competence in skills nor underestimating abilities, which is challenging. Another aspect of ASDs is the lack of ability to interpret gestures, facial expressions and/or body language which we all use constantly when we are interacting with others. If you have never considered this, watch two people holding a conversation and you should be able to understand and translate their likely emotions and feelings from all the visual clues they give out. For many with ASDs this is not a natural skill and will need to be taught. This can also be accompanied by an inability to understand everyday idioms such as 'get your skates on' or 'jump in the bath', which is likely to cause confusion as understanding for many may be literal.

A major difficulty is the lack of knowledge of wider society which can lead to very negative reactions to adults with ASDs. In this age of increasing social inclusion there are still a range of minority groups, including those with ASDs, that are excluded from mainstream society and this needs to be addressed. Increased acceptance within our society should lead to increased inclusion in each of the areas of concern raised by those with ASDs that were raised in earlier chapters: the lack of housing, education, employment, health care and leisure opportunities. Therefore *public awareness strategies should be introduced nationally.*

Chapter 5 considers issues relating to the family members of adolescents and adults with ASDs. It is important that professionals consider the impact of autism on family members. Issues relating to childhood will be discussed at some length, despite this being a text about adolescents and adults with ASDs, as the impact on family members are cumulative throughout life. There is a plethora of personal experiences demonstrating the ongoing battle to secure diagnosis, appropriate education and access to health and social care. When engaging with parents, professionals must be sensitive to the difficulties they may have experienced since the ASD was first acknowledged and diagnosed and do everything in their power to instigate appropriate support that parents have spent so long fighting for. For this reason I have explored issues in childhood at some length to ensure that those who are working with adolescents or adults can be more informed, and thus sensitive, to the struggles the family has already experienced and the long-term impact of these. The difficulties of living with ASDs must also be appreciated as far as possible by the professionals involved as the demands on family members are considerable and should not be dismissed lightly. To assist in our work with family members professionals should have detailed knowledge of all local services and support available and provide useful information, or access to information, to all family members. Again, significant areas of concern for family members are care and support when the parents themselves become too old to provide it, and access to housing, education, health, employment and leisure activities for their grown-up child. Generally speaking all parents desire that their adult child be provided with the appropriate support and provision to enable them to achieve their full potential and lead happy and meaningful lives. Professionals can have either a positive or negative impact on this and we need to ensure it is the former. Hopefully the current Valuing People initiative (DoH, 2001b) will lead to increasing improvements in the future.

Chapter 6 explores a range of intervention approaches that could be considered a basis for ASD-specific provision, although it will be made clear that many professionals utilise a more eclectic approach depending on the needs of the individuals they are working with. The key difficulties experienced by adolescents and adults with ASDs are reflected upon to indicate appropriate strategies to employ, such as using visual approaches to enable those with ASDs to engage with activities. Arguably the most useful source of information on appropriate strategies for any individual is likely to come from the family who will have discovered what does and does not work over the years. Whatever approaches or strategies are used it can be through trial and error that we venture upon a specific strategy that really works for any individual we are working with or caring for. The quality of provision, across the board, should be assessed partly by the ability to provide successfully for those with ASDs, so knowledge of approaches, strategies and positive person-centred planning should be considered by inspection teams.

The importance of early diagnoses and interventions is also emphasised as early intervention strategies should result in early provision which could reduce the level of difficulties later in life. However, it is acknowledged that many parents feel the time delay between diagnosis and provision (at any age) has created more difficulties. Clearly *issues of diagnosis and subsequent provision need to be addressed* to ensure all adolescents and adults with ASDs have access to appropriate diagnoses and provision.

Chapter 7 considers provision in education from secondary school through to educational approaches after leaving school with the transition from children's services to adult services being identified as often unsatisfactory or non-existent (NAS, 2004). *Transition plans must therefore be in place for every young person moving into adulthood* and all those involved with the individual, plus the individual him/herself, should be involved in formulating the transition plan. The final plan should cover all aspects of the individual's life including health, education, employment, leisure and housing and this must be supported through the provision identified within the plan.

Typical difficulties experienced by those with an ASD are explored in depth to indicate useful strategies that should be considered in educational settings such as the layout of teaching space, the need for visual support, potential sensory issues, support with organisational skills, the need for routine and structure, the difficulties posed by large secondary schools at unstructured activity times and, of course, knowledge of ASDs on the part of the staff. Appropriate strategies are highlighted throughout the chapter. Perhaps the most important aspect of educational provision is *identifying potential barriers and working to overcome them, and this will be at the individual student level.*

Chapter 8 considers provision in care settings and the need to empower adults with ASDs to contribute to all decision-making about their needs and desires, and thus their own life. The key changes within the Valuing People strategy (DoH, 2001b) are reflected upon to indicate the ongoing developments that should be taking place in the future. The importance of care plans is also considered as a response to the fact that many adults with ASDs will require some level of support in their adult life. Thus if care plans do not respond appropriately to the needs of the individuals they are intended to support then they become meaningless. Again, person-centred planning approaches and advocacy are highlighted as significant aspects of planning and provision.

As in the previous chapter the key areas of difficulty within adult services, and appropriate strategies to address them, are identified and discussed in Chapter 8 with case studies offered to help link the discussions to real-life situations. This should help the reader to begin developing appropriate practices within their own home or workplace.

The consequences of 'getting it wrong' are discussed briefly to highlight the *absolute necessity to improve services for adults with ASDs as the evidence so far concludes that we are not, currently, addressing ASD needs appropriately.*

Summary

In this book I have tried to work within the current government's philosophy which is striving to improve working across agencies in a more coordinated manner. I have therefore considered provision for adolescents and adults with ASDs across the disciplines of health, education and social care. This, however, presented its own challenges as it is much easier to focus solely on one area of provision. Yet the reality for the people we care for or work with raises issues across all disciplines, so my aim was to address this.

Throughout this book a range of significant issues emerges repeatedly:
- Life for many adolescents and adults with ASDs is complex and confusing.
- All professionals should focus on individual needs as opposed to categories of need.
- All documentation relating to provision for adolescents and adults with learning disabilities or ASDs should utilise the same terminology.
- How can professionals be expected to remain up to date with the vast amount of documentation that is published?
- All legislation should make specific reference to provision for those with ASDs.
- Future policies should be informed by the recommendations of existing reports to ensure the outcomes for adults with ASDs are improved.
- We need to remember that there are many undiagnosed adults.
- We cannot expect staff to instinctively possess knowledge of ASDs, but must, in a coherent manner, ensure they are all trained.
- The most powerful tool we have is our knowledge and understanding of ASDs, the impact they have and how to identify achievable and realistic goals for the future.
- Key areas of concern for adults with ASDs emerge as equality of access to: housing, education, employment, health care and leisure.

- Training for all professionals involved in health, education and/or care is essential if we aim to respond appropriately to the needs of those with ASDs.

- If agencies are expected to work more closely together in a 'seamless' manner then why do we still see documentation emerging from the different agencies? Does this not suggest a contradiction?

- National policies need clearer direction relating to ASDs to ensure ongoing and consistent improvements in provision.

- Awareness of possible sensory issues is essential for all professionals.

- Public awareness strategies should be introduced nationally to address increased inclusion within society.

- Issues of diagnosis and subsequent provision need to be addressed to ensure all adolescents and adults with ASDs have access to appropriate provision.

- Transition plans must be in place for every young person moving into adulthood and at other times, as appropriate.

- Educators should identify potential barriers and work to overcome them at the individual student level.

- Care plans must address all areas of the individual's life, identifying skills achieved, likes, dislikes and needs, and define effective strategies to address each.

- There is an absolute necessity to improve all services for adolescents and adults with ASDs as the evidence so far concludes that we are not, currently, addressing ASD needs appropriately.

As can be seen the issues are considerable but if we reflect on the reality for many adolescents and adults with ASDs and the negative outcomes revealed in reports (Broach et al., 2003; Barnard et al., 2001, 2002, 2003) we can see that steps must be taken to ensure all those with ASDs in our society are provided for appropriately by knowledgeable, trained staff. The challenges are considerable but it is our responsibility to meet them head-on and overcome them as far as possible. It is the individual's right to have choices, to be as independent as possible, to be included and to have their rights acknowledged and met, and it is our duty as professionals and carers to work towards making that happen, empowering those we work with or care for and supporting them to achieve their maximum potential and lead happy and fulfilling lives.

Key issues and suggestions for discussion are offered at the end of each chapter to support the reader. In addition the reader is directed towards further reading relating to the issues explored in the chapter. It is hoped that as you progress through each chapter you will be able to relate each area directly to the adolescents or adults you are working with or caring for. However you use this book, I hope the lives of those you support will be improved and that they themselves may become more empowered.

2

Definitions and the current situation in education, health and social care

This chapter explores:
> definitions of autistic spectrum disorders (ASDs);
> key characteristics and features of ASDs;
> existing provision across education, health and social care services for young people (aged over 16) and adults with ASDs.

Introduction

We are now increasingly living in times where acceptance of difference is more commonplace and education, mainstream secondary schools, further education (FE), higher education (HE) and adult services are expected to provide for the needs of more and more young people and adults (aged 16 years plus) with a range of difficulties who might have previously been placed in special schools or long-term institutions. However, while 'informed' members of society may be more accommodating of adolescents and adults with disabilities we are still a long way off living in a totally inclusive society in which each and every person is accepted and offered every life chance and opportunity to achieve their full potential.

For those adolescents and adults with autistic spectrum disorders (ASDs) life can be complex and confusing. On the one hand a person may be verbally fluent yet on the other hand be unable to go to the corner shop to purchase a few necessities. An ASD is a 'hidden' disability and invariably those with an ASD look just like everyone else but may engage in some very different and unusual behaviours and experience significant social and communication difficulties. To the general public those with ASDs may present as odd, eccentric or even bizarre and their lack of knowledge and ignorance may lead to an internal fear which results in avoidance. Understanding and awareness of ASDs is there-fore crucial in our society to enable increased acceptance of all those with ASDs. Likewise within the education, health and care sectors all staff should have a thorough awareness of the features of ASDs and appropriate methods of support in order to further the lives of those with whom they work.

Special needs, learning difficulties and/or disability

The way our lives work, both personally and professionally, encompasses a need to categorise for a range of purposes, perhaps most significant is the need to have order and structure in our lives. So it has been, over past and present times, that we have developed terms to describe and define ourselves and our lives such as gifted, educated, poor, affluent, tall, short, competent, sensitive, athletic, able-bodied, disabled and so on. What we should never overlook is that we are all individual human beings with individual and unique facets, so we present as a collection of these terms. The government, local authorities and service providers also use categories to clarify provision such as health, social services, education, private, state or voluntary. Within each service are sub-categories that further segregate those involved into allotted boxes, such as mental health difficulties, dyslexic, addiction, in need, truant, residential care and ASD. The planning that then takes place will also be labelled differently, according to the service provider: care plans, care assessments and individual education plans are each discipline specific. However, the adolescents and adults we are focusing on within this book may span several disciplines so common language is imperative to ensure understanding by all involved and also to offer clarity to parents/carers. Whatever we feel about the rights and wrongs of utilising such categories, they are factors in our lives so when refer-ring to adolescents and adults experiencing difficulties accepted terminology will be used throughout this book. People with ASDs will be referred to as such.

Categorising and labelling

If we are to welcome an adult with an ASD into our work setting we may make assumptions regarding their difficulties according to our knowledge and under-standing of ASDs, but this may well deprive or limit the opportunities made available to that adult, thus compounding their difficulties further. In addition the label of autism may limit the range of provision available to that adult to the standard 'set' pathway for those with ASDs, which may well adequately support their needs but may not allow them to develop to their fullest poten-tial. It could therefore be argued that such a pathway does nothing to support increased inclusion within society. On the other hand the label of ASD may well secure increased funding and access to provision not otherwise available, which is clearly a positive aspect. The dilemma is evident.

Current legislation and guidance documents all use terminology specific to their discipline base and this can only lead to increased confusion for all. It also supports the philosophy that special needs provision or provision for those with learning difficulties or disabilities is separate and different from regular provision and as such is exclusive. There exists legislation and guidance for all human beings but then there exists a range of separate documentation for those with special needs, disabilities and/or ASDs. When we can consider all human beings as individuals who each have a range of needs (albeit some more severe than others) which should be provided for appropriately, then we will be nearer to an inclusive society. Should we not be working towards provision for all members of society that automatically accommodates everyone?

Terminology used is therefore often directly linked to provision but when considering appropriate provision for any adolescent or adult experiencing a difficulty it is preferable to start with the individual and explore their strengths and weaknesses, likes and dislikes as well as their areas of specific difficulty. This way our planning and activities are more likely to be individual-specific as opposed to difficulty-specific, which will be implicitly more appropriate and likely to ensure greater success and progress.

Labels and diagnosis

Misdiagnosis is arguably the most disastrous of outcomes as provision is often allocated according to diagnosis. If a 23-year-old male with autism and mental health problems is misdiagnosed as severely mentally ill and unstable he is most likely to be treated for the mental illness. If the staff working with him are not aware of the autism and its effects then any treatment is unlikely to address all his difficulties appropriately and, at worst, treatment may compound his difficulties further. Peeters (1997: 7) concluded that: 'This is not how it should be, but it is still the case that the quality of an autistic person's life depends more on the place where he was born and whether it is a place where autism is properly understood.' So while we acknowledge the importance and value of diagnosis we must ensure diagnoses result in positive provision.

A further issue arises when diagnosing adults with ASDs as questioning the adult will, quite rightly, be involved. The very nature of ASD informs us that conversations may create incredible difficulties for someone with an ASD and to bring the questioning to a speedy conclusion adults may well answer what they think will make the professional end the process or just answer 'yes' to everything. Their understanding may be severely restricted so any responses must be interpreted within the context of the individual's conversational and linguistic abilities. Their understanding is also predominantly literal so questions must be presented in an unambiguous manner to support understanding. Howlin (2004: 284) illustrates this effectively:

> If someone with autism is asked a standard diagnostic question, such as 'Do you ever hear voices when no one else is in the same room?', most will answer 'Yes' – for of course we *all* hear voices when people are not actually in the same

room. This failure to interpret the underlying meaning of the question is likely to lead to a positive response by someone with autism, even though there is no real evidence of delusions or hallucinations.

Paranoid behaviours can also be misinterpreted when in fact it is the adult's lack of ability to cope with a life that is riddled with confusion and contradiction that results in clinical depression and paranoia. The aggression can be a result of the depression and/or their reaction to failing to cope – either of which can be the result of the ASD. Until the root problem (the ASD) is addressed there is unlikely to be significant progress and in the meantime the adult may be supported by those unaware of the ASD and thus engaging in inappropriate strategies.

Alternatively, however, accurate diagnosis can lead to appropriate provision and can help those with ASDs to understand their own behaviour more readily. This can also be a positive support for their families. Wendy Lawson, well known as a writer and lecturer who has Asperger syndrome, relays clearly how her misdiagnosis of 'intellectually disabled and schizophrenic' caused her significant problems for many years and only when Asperger syndrome was diagnosed did she truly begin to understand her own behaviours more appropriately and put in place appropriate strategies to support herself and her life more positively (Lawson, 2000, 2002). Clearly the key issue is that accurate diagnoses are essential for those with ASDs.

A further issue to consider is that of consent for assessment and diagnosis from the adult with ASD themselves. Current UK legislation and policy make it clear that everyone should agree to any process or intervention they are to be a part of, but do we allow all adults with ASDs this right and offer them support?

Professionals are under increasing pressure to validate, justify and evidence every aspect of their work and at the same time service users are becoming more proactive in their fight for equality and improved services. As a result our provision needs to accept these changes and find ways to move forwards. Arguably for adolescents and adults with ASDs the most significant and basic change needed is increased understanding and knowledge of ASDs by society and all professionals responsible for service delivery. Sadly, until this occurs, professionals are likely to continue compounding the difficulties for their service users through ignorance, a situation we clearly need to resolve.

Autism and Asperger syndrome

Prior to being identified as a unique disability ASDs were considered within the realms of mental illness and at one point children with ASD-like symptoms were considered to be the recipients of 'frigid parenting' wherein they received little or no love and attention from their main carers. As a result they withdrew from the world for fear of further rejection and became aloof and lone individuals. This belief was held by both Kanner and Bettleheim but was soon disputed by other eminent scientists and researchers. Once Kanner's later work emerged in the 1940s and the term 'early infantile autism' was introduced into medical terminology, clarification of the differences between autism and other mental illnesses was established. Wing (1976), however, suggested that Kanner's reference to early infantile autism was 'inappropriate' as it implied the onset of autism in infancy. In reality for many children onset is during their second or third year so 'early childhood autism' could be more appropriate.

Asperger's work then followed identifying a separate group of children with similar symptoms to the group with autism, but with some significant differences and hence Asperger syndrome became recognised.

Bernard Rimland had experienced autism first-hand as his son was diagnosed with the disability. Rimland established the Autism Society of America and his first work to have major impact was to question the theory of frigid parenting as he gathered evidence from experience and research highlighting the possibility of a biological theory of autism. His ongoing work in the field continues to inform policy and practice.

From the start of the 1950s concerns emerged in Europe and the United States regarding provision for children with disabilities and at the same time changes in society were evolving producing a more caring and politically aware people who began to fight for their rights and against injustice, both as individuals and as powerful groups. Since then campaigning groups for disabilities and ASDs have continued to emerge and parents have also become a powerful force to make representation to policy-makers as well as being more involved in the provision arrangements and development of their child or adult son or daughter. In the 1960s and 1970s intervention approaches also began to emerge for a range of disabilities, including ASDs, such as the Lovaas approach and TEACCH (Treatment and Education of Communication Handicapped Children). It was also during the 1960s that the Society for Autistic Children was created (now the National Autistic Society – NAS) by a group of parents who felt that appropriate care and support was not available.

Autism, as with many other conditions and disorders, is individual and manifests in different ways in different people. However, as a lifelong developmental disability autism was considered to be an extreme mental disorder until Kanner's work in the United States culminating in his paper of 1943 characterising 'early infantile autism'. He identified there were some similarities between the characteristics of autism and other existing conditions but highlighted several unique features:

- Lack of desire to communicate verbally
- Echolalic verbal utterances
- Fear in strange or unexpected situations
- Lack of imaginative play activities
- Repetitive behaviours demonstrated. (Wall, 2004: 6)

At the same time Hans Asperger was developing his own research in Austria identifying similar difficulties and characteristics but focusing more on individuals with greater ability. Interestingly both Kanner and Asperger were born in Austria but Kanner emigrated to the United States in his late twenties to pursue a career in child psychiatry. Asperger's work identified the same fundamental difficulties but also highlighted differences with milder impairments, reduced language delays, higher IQs and increased adaptability (Siegel, 1996; Howlin 2004).

Triad of impairments

Three classic areas of difficulty (the triad of impairments) which should all occur for a diagnosis, are evident in everyday life for those with autism (see Figure 2.1). These areas of difficulty are:

• social interaction

• social communication

• imagination.

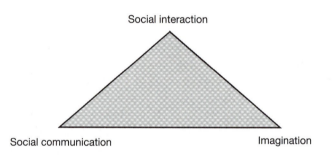

Figure 2.1 The triad of impairments

Impairments in one or more of these areas would not, in itself, warrant an ASD diagnosis but all three must have been present by the age of three years. It is important to extend our knowledge and understanding of ASDs so that all those with ASDs can be supported appropriately. Effective and thorough planning, informed by regular observation, will support this process.

The DfES/DoH document *Autistic Spectrum Disorders: Good Practice Guidance* (2002b: 6) offers a description of ASDs which although relating to children incorporates the key features:

... all children with an ASD share a triad of impairments in their ability to:

• understand and use non-verbal communication

- understand social behaviour which affects their ability to interact with children and adults

- think and behave flexibly – which may be shown in restricted, obsessional or repetitive activities.

Some children with an ASD have a different perception of sounds, sights, smells, touch and taste, which affects their responses to these sensations. They may also have unusual sleep and behaviour patterns and behavioural problems. Children of all levels of ability can have an ASD and it can occur with other disorders (for example, with sensory loss or Down's syndrome).

Prevalence

Prevalence figures are always subject to ongoing change but in general we know that ASDs are now more frequently diagnosed. This does not necessarily relate to increases in the numbers of people with ASDs but is more likely to be related to improved diagnostic processes, knowledge and understanding. There are also complications within the diagnostic processes due to coexisting conditions that may predominate so the autism may be overlooked, and further issues surround the similarities and differences between classic autism, Asperger syndrome or even non-pervasive developmental disorder – not otherwise specified (PDD-NOS). The skills of the diagnostic professional will be paramount in securing an accurate diagnosis (Siegel, 1996).

In 2003 the National Autistic Society identified a rate of 90 per 10,000 people, taking into account the whole spectrum of ASDs (Wall, 2004), but currently they are suggesting 1 in 100. Figures also suggest that classic autism is more likely in boys than girls, with a ratio of 4 : 1. For any professional working with adolescents and adults it must be assumed that they are very likely to be working with someone with an ASD during their career, and for some it will be many more. More recently, a study by Baird of Guy's and St Thomas's NHS Foundation Trust examined rates of ASDs in around 57,000 children aged nine to ten and concluded that 38.9 per 10,000 had autism, 77.2 per 100,000 for other ASDs and 116.1 per 10,000 for total ASDs (Baird, 2006).

Clearly this holds implications for those working with adolescents and adults as the numbers progressing through to adulthood and thus needing services will increase substantially over the coming years. This issue has been raised within the NAS report *Tomorrow's Big Problem* (Harker and King, 2004: 16):

> It is abundantly clear that all local area services will need to plan for these increased levels of demand on already over-stretched existing services and consider the impact on current practice of service delivery.

Key features of autism and Asperger syndrome

The main distinguishing features between autism and Asperger syndrome are the presence of relatively average cognitive skills and the lack of early language delay in the Asperger group.

Wing (1991) offers clarity of understanding:

Kanner's autism – key features:

- Lack of desire for contact with others
- Obsessive resistance to change
- Fascination for objects
- Lack of meaningful verbal language
- Ability to complete performance tests or memory skills
- Impairment of non-verbal aspects of communication
- Some aspects of physical agility yet lack of coordination with some basic physical skills
- Stereotyped movements (rocking, toe-walking, flapping)
- Unusual responses to sensory stimuli
- Lack of ability to imitate
- Feeding difficulties
- Temper outbursts and aggressiveness ignorant of their effects on others.

Asperger additional features:

- Speech before school age
- Social isolation yet awareness of others
- Inappropriate social behaviours
- In-depth knowledge of some areas, occasionally with little obvious use
- Odd in appearance.

(adapted from Wing, 1991: 95–7)

The reality for adolescents and adults with ASDs

In today's society there will be many adolescents and adults who either received a late diagnosis or remain undiagnosed. Able to attend mainstream schools they may have adapted their own coping strategies to overcome their difficulties and due to their attention to detail those with ASDs may have performed extremely well in some curriculum areas. Additionally, their lack of social appropriateness will make it difficult for them to engage meaningfully in the social aspects of education and will probably have led them to being more focused on their academic work.

Perhaps continuing in education through to A level studies/sixth form college, further education (FE) or into higher education (HE), such successful individuals may then secure places at HE level, proceeding to graduate in their chosen studies. In my own experience, young adults with ASDs do, however, struggle greatly with the changes from their previous school and the expectations of FE/HE, as well as the social side of FE/HE life, particularly for those living away from home. Knowledgeable and caring tutors will be essential to offer appropriate and ongoing support for both academic and non-academic issues. Yet how many lecturers, senior lecturers and principal lecturers are likely to have a working knowledge of ASDs? Whitaker (2001: 7–8) suggests the following difficulties as typical for those with ASDs:

- being frightened or stressed by contact with other people
- being bothered about pleasing other people/making friends
- causing offence without realising/appearing insensitive
- misunderstanding people's intentions
- going too far without realising
- not knowing how to react to other people's feelings
- forming and keeping friendships
- keeping a conversation going
- knowing if another person is interested
- being able to read body language/tone of voice
- being able to tell if someone means what they are saying.

Much can be learnt from listening to those adolescents and adults that have experienced secondary education FE, HE and employment as they are most likely to offer truly informed suggestions for improvements within the institutions as well as strategies for those with ASDs to use. Professionals should not make assumptions on behalf of individuals with ASDs but should involve them in decision-making relating to their own, appropriate support. Morgan (1998) offers insights into the world of employment for those with ASDs, such as the example of a man with autism writing an article for his work colleagues explaining the differences between his own behaviours and those of his workmates in the hope they would be more aware and understanding of him. While we rightly need to ensure our work with and for those with ASDs is appropriate we should not overlook the difficulties that have been experienced by, and in many cases are continuing to affect, the individuals and their families.

For those less able adolescents and adults the picture can look very different and while many texts will explore the difficulties experienced by more able individuals, offering strategies to support their development and progress for the individuals, professionals and families, we need to address all issues for all individuals. The NAS report *Ignored or Ineligible: The Reality for Adults with Autistic Spectrum Disorders'* highlights some significant facts and issues for us all to reflect upon:

- Only 38% of people with autism and Asperger syndrome have a community care assessment. Only 16% were actually offered one; others had to fight for one. Only 45% are actually receiving the services specified in the assessment.

- At the point of transition from adolescence to adulthood a little over half of families (53%) had a transition plan in place. Only 16% have had their identified needs met in full.

- 18% of lower functioning adults were not diagnosed until beyond the age of 16 whilst 46% of people with Asperger syndrome were not diagnosed until over the age of 16.

- 59% agreed that responsibility for funding and providing care and support fell between agencies.

- ASDs constantly fall through the gap between mental health and learning disability.

- 70% of parents felt their son/daughter would be unable to live independently and less than 10% can manage the most basic household tasks such as shopping, preparing meals, paying bills, laundry …

- Only 12% of higher functioning adults are in full-time paid employment.

- 65% of parents said their sons and daughters had difficulty making friends and 72% said their son or daughter had behaviours which other people find unusual or anti-social.

- 32% of parents reported that their son or daughter had experienced mental ill health. 56% had suffered with depression, a further 11% a nervous breakdown and 8% felt suicidal or had attempted suicide.   (Barnard et al., 2001: 6–7)

Clearly this is not a picture of an inclusive society that provides effectively for its members with ASDs and this is a situation that must be addressed as a matter of urgency. When this is considered beyond the human costs we discover significant issues such as the emotional, physical and economic costs to the families and individuals themselves, as well as the estimated costs through life for a person with an ASD: £2,940,538 (Knapp and Jarbrink, 2001).

Developments in education

Since the Education Act of 1944 (Ministry of Education, 1944) when special education was first addressed in legislation, educational provision has undergone progressive changes. Prior to this time diagnoses and subsequent provision were within the remit of health professionals but as from 1944 the responsibility was passed to local education authorities (LEAs). Through the steady expansion of special school provision from the 1950s onwards we have recently experienced a turnaround in policy and many of these special schools are now being closed down with increasing numbers of pupils being accommodated in mainstream schools in a move towards greater inclusion for all pupils. Each school has a special educational needs coordinator (SENCO) who has responsibility for coordinating the special provision in the school and ensuring staff are able to support the children within the establishment appropriately. Governed by the SEN Code of Practice (DfES, 2001b) they ensure the staged approach is activated when a student of concern is highlighted. The student is placed on *School Action* and special support is set in place to help them achieve success and move forwards. If this is unsuccessful or little progress is made the child would be moved to *School Action Plus* which could culminate in a Statutory Assessment of their needs and a Statement of Special Educational Needs. Parents are seen as partners throughout this process. Teachers working with children with ASDs can utilise the *Autistic Spectrum Disorders: Good Practice Guidance* (DfES, 2002b), referred to earlier in this chapter, but in my own experience during training for practising teachers I was saddened to discover that the majority had not heard of or seen this useful publication.

Children with special needs should hopefully be accommodated within their local mainstream provision but those who are unable to cope in mainstream settings can be placed in a range of special units, special schools or schools solely for children with ASDs, although these are few and far between and are thus not available to all.

Over the years teachers have been able to access training on a range of educational issues but within initial teacher training there can be a distinct lack of input regarding provision for children with special educational needs, let alone children with ASDs. This being the case how can we ensure that all teachers of young people with ASDs in secondary education can understand their needs and difficulties and provide appropriate activities and support to ensure success? Howlin (2004: 182) supports the need for specialist training for all teachers.

All young people within secondary education (11 years +) will follow the National Curriculum which encourages teachers to 'modify' programmes of study to ensure all pupils, including those with special needs, are able to access appropriate learning opportunities. For children with severe and complex needs head teachers have the authority to 'disapply' the National Curriculum as appropriate. The subjects to be taught are laid down, with English, Mathematics, Science, ICT, Physical Education and Citizenship being compulsory at every stage of education.

In 2005 the Education and Skills White Paper set up planned reforms for the education of 14–19 year olds, aiming to broaden options for learners, to establish a rise in those staying in education till 18 years of age and to try to re-engage disaffected students. All students aged 13–19, and for those up to 25 if they have learning difficulties or disabilities, have access to a local Connexions Service which offers personal advisers who can give: 'information, advice and practical help with all sort of things that might be affecting you at school, college or work or in your personal or family life' (Internet 3).

From the age of 16 the young person's future options begin to expand as they may continue with education into sixth-form college, FE or HE or leave school and progress into the world of work. The Connexions service and/or careers department at school will be able to advise their choices at this juncture. If continuing in education the student with special needs may attend the local FE college for life skills classes or, for the more academically able, a range of courses will be available. Similarly at HE level a range of higher academic courses will be available. Within FE and HE institutions students with ASDs can be supported by Disability Officers who offer support and advice on all aspects of student life (academic and personal). Knowledgeable academic tutors can also be allocated to students with ASDs to support their academic studies and, equally, student study support services are available to support students. Yet this depends on those tutors having ASD knowledge.

Developments in health and social care

Historically people with learning disabilities or mental health problems were likely to be detained in depressing institutions where only the basic food and accommodation needs were met, often being called 'imbeciles' or 'mad'.

The NHS came into being in 1948 when medical technologies and treatments were beginning to see changes and improvements for the treatment and care of patients. The original NHS was divided into three parts:

- Hospitals
- Family doctors, dentists, opticians and pharmacists
- Local authority health services, community nursing, midwifery, health visiting, maternal and infant welfare clinics, immunisations and the control of infectious diseases. (Internet 4)

During subsequent years the NHS has undergone considerable change and continues to outspend the financial budget awarded it. However, for young people and adults with ASDs the current situation should mean easier access to GPs for general health needs and referrals to specialist services and to dentists and opticians. Welfare benefits also support those with disabilities to enable them to lead more fulfilling lives and to secure medicines and treatments as well as supporting living allowances. From the evolution of the NHS until quite recently consistent changes have occurred but these have generally related to funding and budget holding control, or the expansion or restructuring and/or amalgamation of NHS trusts to reduce costs. The actual services available to the public have continued to expand and more specialist hospital facilities now exist, which are a result of improving knowledge, science and technology enabling more advanced techniques to be developed.

Perhaps the most significant development in health of late is the Every Child Matters initiative (DfES, 2004a), applying to all children, young people and families. This innovative and far reaching initiative sets out to 'provide the national framework for 150 local programmes of change to be led by local authorities and their partners' (Internet 5) and is based around five key outcomes for all children and young people:

1 Being healthy

2 Staying safe

3 Enjoying and achieving

4 Making a positive contribution

5 Achieving economic well-being.

Focusing on proactive early intervention as opposed to reactive intervention processes the Children Act 2004 gives the legislative foundation for the implementation of change. Also integral to Every Child Matters is the National Service Framework (NSF) for Children, Young People and Maternity Services (DoH, 2004a) whereby all agencies working with families will work within a Common Assessment Framework aimed at improving inter-agency working for the benefit of all children, young people and their families. A ten-year strategy, the NSF includes eleven standards which should be met by the year 2014. Standard 8 refers specifically to those with disabilities and defines the quality of services that should be developed by 2014:

> Children and young people who are disabled or who have complex health needs receive coordinated, high-quality child and family-centred services which are based on assessed needs, which promote social inclusion and, where possible, which enable them and their families to live ordinary lives.
>
> (DoH, 2004a: 7)

This is an ambitious target for professionals and decision-makers to meet but there is a hint of realism in the statement as it states 'where possible', so one could argue this is the 'get-out' clause. In 2005 the ECM agenda was followed by Youth Matters (Her Majesty's Government, 2005a: 1) which aims:

> ... to make sure that all young people are given the best chance in life to succeed – by improving their qualifications, getting better jobs and making positive contributions to their local communities.

The Children's Trusts at local levels will be responsible for producing a range of appropriate activities to engage young people and offer them a more successful future to reduce the numbers of disaffected adolescents. This initiative extends to cover further help to those young people who are over 16 years of age 'to help think through post-16 options, personal and health issues and career choices' (ibid., p. 8).

Young people with disabilities receive scant reference within this strategy: 'Young people with disabilities tell us that they want to be able to take part in the same range of activities and opportunities as any other young person but they encounter additional barriers to access' (DfES, 2006: 2.16). A range of strategies are proposed to ensure greater participation for those with disabilities, all to be implemented by 2008.

Care services

Young people in residential care are perhaps some of the most disadvantaged in the country as they will already have experienced upheaval, upset and possibly severe trauma, which may have resulted in a range of behaviours of a behavioural, psychological, social, emotional, physical or cognitive nature that have created problems for them in their everyday lives. For a variety of reasons a young person with an ASD may be placed into care, be adopted or placed in a residential children's home, therefore the staff/carers will need to have knowledge and understanding of issues relating to ASDs to be able to provide appropriate support. If they do not have this knowledge they could inadvertently be compounding their difficulties further. The National Autism Plan for Children (NAS, 2003: 48), although referring to young children up to age seven only, recommended that 'Each local area should develop a multi-agency coordinating group that will oversee development of ASD services' and continued that local area training in ASD should be available to all community groups. To ensure the quality of services for adolescents and adults with ASDs it could be suggested that these issues are relevant for all people of all ages with ASDs, for if we fail to provide appropriately for the younger children how can we expect to pick up the pieces later when their difficulties are likely to be compounded?

Within care services we currently have a range of housing options for young people and adults with autism. For the under 16 age group the adolescents are likely to be in their own family homes or other family homes (if fostered, adopted or on a very short-term placement) or residential homes run by the local council. However, when councils have insufficient places in their own care homes they often secure placements at private care homes. Care work is renowned for being underrated and underpaid and in my own experience the qualifications of staff may be limited, so for private care homes that cater for young people with learning difficulties (which are constantly increasing in numbers) the knowledge of learning difficulties among the staff may be limited. This clearly needs to be addressed, possibly through a nationwide training programme for all such care workers. For the over 16 age group with ASDs the following housing and options are available:

- *Sheltered housing* – where residents can live in flats, bungalows or shared houses but are supported by a warden, either living-in or on call.

- *Council homes* – following assessment by the council adults with special needs may have the opportunity of securing a council house, flat or bungalow, to enable independent living.

- *Care homes (council or privately owned)* – for respite care or longer-term placements. Staff will work on a rota system and there is always a member of staff present during the night. All registered care homes are inspected by the Commission for Social Care Inspection (CSCI).

• *Support within their own homes from specialist carers and/or nurses.*

In 2003 the Supporting People programme evolved which funds, plans and monitors housing support services. The programme:

> ... provides housing related support to help vulnerable people to live as independently as possible in the community, whether in their own homes or in hostels, sheltered housing or other specialised supported housing. Supporting People only funds housing support but this can be part of a package of differently funded but co-ordinated support which meets the needs of individuals.

(Internet 6)

Summary

Education, health and social care have progressed away from Victorian institutional life for adolescents and adults with severe learning difficulties, mental health issues and/or ASDs to more community-based provision. The quality of the provision offered, however, will vary and may or may not meet the needs of those with ASDs effectively. Training, and therefore funding to support it – will be essential if we aim to ensure the individual needs of adolescents and adults with ASDs can be met and each individual is supported and motivated to make consistent progress and aim for greater independence. As we will see in Chapter 3 a raft of legislation, guidance and reports has been published over recent years to support progress in this crucial area.

For any professionals or carers wishing to secure a diagnosis it would be useful to use the Autism Screening for Adults checklist available on the NAS website to inform the decision.

Key issues

❖ There is now a multitude of legislation, guidance and government initiatives to support our work with adolescents and adults with ASDs, but much of this is generic, referring to learning difficulties or disabilities rather than relating specifically to provision and support for ASDs.

❖ Training is essential for *all* those working with people with ASDs. This has funding implications.

❖ Lack of training is likely to result in appropriate support which may compound the difficulties already being experienced.

❖ Outcomes for adults with ASDs are not generally good and the government should consider the recommendations made within key reports to inform future policy.

❖ A National Autism Plan for Adults is essential (as drafted by the NAS).

Suggestions for discussion (professionals)

1. With your colleagues discuss the collective knowledge of ASDs and whether ASD training is needed.

2. If training needs are identified find ways to make it happen.

Suggestions for discussion (parents)

1. If your son or daughter attends a school, college and/or care setting, find out how knowledgeable staff are regarding ASDs and how to support your son/daughter.

2. How can you, as a parent, influence the policy and practices within your son/daughter's placement? What mechanisms are in place to enable communication and discussion? If you are unsure as to the answers to these questions consider finding ways to improve the situation. Perhaps consider working with other parents if you share similar issues.

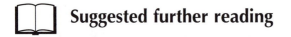 **Suggested further reading**

Howlin, P. (2004) *Autism and Aspergers Syndrome: Preparing for Adulthood.* 2nd edition. London: Routledge. (Chapters 1 and 2)

Jordan, R. (1999) *Autistic Spectrum Disorders: An Introductory Handbook for Practitioners.* London: David Fulton. (Chapter 1)

Wall, K. (2004) *Autism and Early Years Practice.* London: Paul Chapman. (Chapter 1)

3

Policy developments, legislation and guidance

This chapter explores:
➤ historical developments relating to adolescents and adults with learning difficulties and/or ASDs;
➤ current legislation and guidance;
➤ consideration of human rights and disability discrimination issues.

A timeline of significant legislation is offered at the end of this chapter.

Introduction

While it could be perceived as 'easier' to catalogue education developments, then proceed to health, then social care, they will be considered in chronological order within one multi-agency framework, as with the philosophy of this text. Current developments demand increased collaborative working and for all professionals to consider the 'wider' picture that is the individual, their environments and all professionals supporting them. Through developing this chapter I have been able to see the 'coming together' of all agencies more clearly and I hope readers will share this experience.

Since the 1990s we have experienced a deluge of documentation relating to education, health and social care and are currently experiencing major changes across all sectors. Through considering each, the speed of change should become clear but this raises the question of how all professionals can be expected to become familiar with each of these important areas and the changes they must implement. So should we expect professionals simply to effect required changes without allowing a period of time to grasp and reflect on their aims and underlying principles?

Early provision

Prior to the identification of autism as a specific condition those with ASDs would have been likely to be classified as imbeciles, idiots or feeble-minded and later as mentally handicapped, due to the lack of understanding of their specific behaviours and areas of difficulty. They would therefore have been provided for in the same manner as people with mental difficulties or learning disabilities. Early legislation focused more on the perceived dangers such people posed to society as opposed to how best to support them:

• Poor Law Commission 1833

• Lunacy Act/Insanity Act 1845

• Lunatic Asylums Act 1853

• Lunatics Amendment Act 1862

• Idiots Act 1886. (McClimens, 2005)

Once individuals were placed in long-stay hospital or workhouse type accommodation their rights were non-existent and their voices were not to be heard so they remained 'silent and invisible' (Atkinson, 2005: 9). Alongside this segregative legislation Forster's Education Act of 1870 was passed offering education to all children for the first time, including those who were previously perceived as ineducable (Wall, 2006).

In the 1890s, local authorities were required to make provision for all blind and deaf children, and were given the option to provide for 'mentally defective' children. After the Boer War it became apparent that the health and fitness of the armed forces were of an unacceptably low standard creating national concern. As a result the 1909 Education Act introduced school meals and medical inspections in an attempt to improve the situation nationally. Intelligence tests were also introduced (Wall, 2006).

The Mental Deficiency Act of 1913 created four categories of learning difficulties: 'feeble-minded', 'idiots', imbeciles' and 'moral defectives' (Richardson, 2005: 73), terms which today would be considered extremely offensive. At this time there was a movement to rid society of such individuals so long-term internment was seen as the safest option for all concerned.

In 1942 the Beveridge Report highlighted many of the welfare concerns of the time which were linked to national economic stability and aimed to ensure increased support for the more vulnerable members of society (Jones, 2000). Soon after, the 'welfare state' emerged with the fundamental principle of securing the national economy but subsequent changes in government have meant it has not always been a smooth journey of progress. In the late 1960s and 1970s there was an economic slump and the gap between the economically stable and the poor increased substantially creating doubts about the efficacy of the welfare system.

The Education Act emerged in 1944 stating that LEAs 'should have regard to the need for securing that provision is made for pupils who suffer from any disability of mind and body by providing special educational treatment' (Ministry of Education, 1944: 5). The Handicapped Pupils and School Health Regulations of 1945 highlighted eleven categories of disability:

1 Blind

2 Partially blind

3 Deaf

4 Partially deaf

5 Delicate

6 Diabetic

7 Educationally subnormal

8 Epileptic

9 Maladjustment

10 Physically handicapped

11 Speech defects.

Diagnosis would be undertaken by medical professionals and children were placed in the special school that was deemed most appropriate for their difficulties.

In 1948 we saw the advent of the National Health Service (NHS) in the UK and, once established, funding was transferred from the government to local health authorities; they, in turn, delegated the funding to the hospitals within their responsibility. General practitioners (GPs) received direct funding based on the number of patients on their lists and capital costs (Talbot-Smith and Pollock, 2006). Alongside these developments in health, social care provision also emerged provided by local welfare services.

During the 1950s and 1960s parents began to express their dissatisfaction with existing educational services and started to demand more appropriate provision for their children within a system that avoided having to fit into one of the eleven categories of disability. As a result the Education (Handicapped Children) Act (DES, 1970) placed special educational provision within the remit of the local education authority and special schools were established for children with special needs.

In 1971 the White Paper *Better Services for the Mentally Handicapped* was published instigating the start of the closure of long-stay institutions. Their replacement with a preference for community-based care programmes created some hostility from neighbourhood community groups.

At this point developments were seen relating to disability rights as the United Nations Convention on the Rights of Mentally Retarded Persons 1971 emerged stating that those affected '... shall enjoy the right to proper care; education; rehabilitation; guidance; economic security; work to the fullest extent possible; family life; protection from exploitation and abuse; and proper proce-dure to be adopted before any deprivation of rights' (Brammer, 2005: 91). This addressed the needs of people experiencing mental health difficulties for the first time.

In 1976 the Court Report was produced highlighting the need for screening of health and development in the early years (0–5 years) to identify difficulties earlier and set in place appropriate provision which was hoped would reduce the need for provision into adulthood. The Warnock Report (DES, 1978) emerged two years later following a comprehensive study of educational provi-sion for 'handicapped children and young people'. Hailed as innovative at that time the report informed subsequent legislation and significantly changed the face of special education, stating that we should be 'committed to educating them, as a matter of right and to developing their full potential' (ibid.: 1.11). The report suggested a five-stage approach to provision in schools beginning with the identification of difficulties and working though support to ameliorate those difficulties. If further support was deemed necessary then the child could be assessed resulting in a Statement of Special Needs clarifying the child's diffi-culties and the provision needed to meet these needs. Parental partnerships were also deemed crucial to the process. In 1981 the Education Act (DES, 1981) legislated for many of Warnock's recommendations and defined the term special educational needs:

Children have a learning difficulty if:

- they have significantly greater difficulty in learning than the majority of children of their age, or
- they have a disability which prevents or hinders them from making use of the educational facilities generally provided in schools, for children of their age.

[it continued] that a child has a learning difficulty if he/she:

- has a learning disability which requires educational provision that is additional to, or otherwise different from, the educational provision made generally avail-able within the school, or:
- if he/she has a physical disability.   (DES, 1981: s.1.1)

The key features of the 1981 Act were:

- Focus to be placed on individual needs rather than categories of need.
- Provision for children with special educational needs to become the responsi-bility of the LEA.
- All categories of handicap were removed.
- Effective parental partnerships should be established.
- Integration should occur wherever practicable.   (DES, 1981: s.1.1)

So we were now moving towards an educational system that recognised individual needs as opposed to specific conditions and teachers were encouraged to address individual needs rather than offer generic support. With this clearer focus on individual needs, provision for young people with ASDs may have experienced some improvements within schools, but there were still many teachers (as there are today) who did not have adequate understanding of how to provide for young people with ASDs.

In and after 1979, when Margaret Thatcher was elected as Prime Minister, both health and social services experienced considerable change (Jones and Tucker, 2000). A move towards contract working in health was established whereby hospitals and GPs commissioned specific services they required in a bid to command the best prices and thus improve services. Similarly every local social services department commissioned 'care packages' for their clients (Jones and Tucker, 2000). These changes were instigated by the *Caring for People* (DoH, 1989) and *Community Care: Agenda for Action* (DoH, 1988) initiatives. In 1983, via the Mental Health Act (DoH, 1983), definitions of 'mental health' emerged to clarify this particular range of difficulties: 'mental illness, arrested or incomplete development of mind, psychopathic disorder and any other disorder or disability of mind' (Brammer, 2005: 92). Within social care the increased community care resulted in major demands on social services budgets which led to gross overspending. While ensuring more community-based provision for thousands of people it was clear that fundamental budgetary issues needed addressing, but to suddenly halt or limit funding to private groups would have been disastrous, resulting in many closures and insufficient placements for the residents. Leading up to an election, it could be argued that the governing party did not want to cause more unrest at this time. The outcome at the time was for a mixed economy of private and public funding and provision.

Although by the 1980s ASDs were increasingly being recognised, diagnoses were somewhat limited and accuracy could not be assured. Yet within the existing definitions of education and health it was still not clear how provision would be decided upon and what the characteristics of appropriate provision were. This was to come later. In the 1960s and 1970s adolescents and adults with ASDs would have been predominantly cared for in the same ways as those with mental health issues or psychiatric disorders requiring special provision. Many children, young people and adults with ASDs were likely to have been diagnosed with 'childhood psychosis' (Howlin, 2004: 21) and the majority were likely to have been placed in special schools or long-stay hospitals or institutions while others would have been able to lead fairly independent lives. Appropriate provision was not prevalent – again due to lack of knowledge and training.

Returning to history

The Children Act of 1989 brought together all preceding legislation regarding the welfare of children and further definitions emerged:

A child shall be taken as 'in need' if:

he is unlikely to achieve or maintain, or to have the opportunity of achieving or maintaining, a reasonable standard of health or development without the provision for him of services by a local authority under this Part;

his health or development is likely to be significantly impaired, or further impaired, without the provision for him of such services; or,

he is disabled.   (DoH, 1991: s. 2.3)

At this point, both working with parents and working in partnership with other agencies were becoming fundamental issues in all emerging reports, guidance and legislation and the Children Act also placed a strong emphasis on these aspects of professional practice (Anderson-Ford, 1994).

The National Health Services and Community Care Act (DoH, 1990) legislated for the changes that were strongly debated during the 1980s. The Audit Commission's report *Making a Reality of Community Care* (Audit Commission, 1986) presented a scathing attack on the existing NHS service:

It was a cogent and highly critical document. It discussed the fragmented nature of the so-called spectrum of care that was supposed to be available from hospital to domiciliary care. It pointed out that many agencies were involved and that many people were either getting the wrong kind of care or not getting care at all.   (Lewis and Glennister, 2000: 33)

The Act was passed to solve a range of issues such as the increasing numbers of older citizens who were admitted to hospitals for temporary illnesses or fractures and who could not be released due to the lack of supportive care within their own communities. Key points included:

• assessments of need were instigated;
• services offered should be clearly mapped to individual needs;
• hospitals became self-managing 'trusts'.

This new model of providing services was established 'in which the underlying assumption was that separating purchasers and providers would bring better value for money and increase accountability and efficiency' (Jones and Tucker, 2000: 6).

Educational provision for young people with special educational needs had also been undergoing further changes as a result of the gaps and problems that emerged as a result of the implementation of the 1981 Education Act. Lindsay (1997: 20) stated that: 'The Act was inconsistent, inefficient and clearly did not meet the objective of ensuring each child with SEN received a quality assessment, and provision to meet the needs identified.' Many parents were dissatisfied with the services offered to their children and the lack of appropriateness of those services, and during the 1980s parents' campaigning groups began to emerge, such as 'Network 81'. As a result the 1993 Education Act (DfEE, 1993) was passed, followed by the Code of Practice (DfEE, 1994) which:

...offered LEAs and practitioners very clear and specific guidelines on all aspects of special educational needs provision including:

- identification of SEN;
- assessment of SEN;
- a new five-staged assessment process culminating in a statement of SEN;
- regular reviews of progress, provision and statements;
- the introduction of the special educational needs coordinator (SENCO).

(Wall, 2006: 20)

In 1995 the Disability Discrimination Act (HMSO, 1995) was passed giving people with disabilities increased rights to provision as they generally have increased health, education and social care needs than the average population. This legislation has since been updated (Disability Discrimination Act 2005).

So we now begin to see considerable changes within all sectors of provision. More diagnoses of ASDs were secured and more appropriate provision to address educational needs was emerging for some. The role of the SENCO who would oversee all special educational needs provision would have been pivotal, and thus that person's knowledge and understanding of ASDs would have being crucial. However, we now realise that the needs of adolescents and adults with ASDs regarding education, health and social care issues were still not being met at that time. The beginnings of progress were taking place but this was generic as opposed to ASD specific.

Returning to history again

Within the field of health, Primary Care Trusts (replacing Primary Care Groups) were established following the 1997 White Paper *The New NHS. Modern, Dependable* (Talbot-Smith and Pollock, 2006). Their purpose is summarised:

> The role of PCTs is to improve the health of the community, to secure high quality, primary, secondary and community care services, and to integrate local health and social care services. This makes them responsible for commissioning, or overseeing the commissioning by GP practices, of the full range of healthcare and community services for their local populations. (ibid. 2006: 37)

Following the 1971 White Paper *Better Services for the Mentally Handicapped* a steady system of closing more and more long-stay hospitals began in an attempt to replace institutional care with more locally based and personal residential care provision. Yet for many young people in such hospitals the closure did not come around until 2001. For adolescents and adults with mild or moderate learning disabilities, the move into sheltered accommodation or shared/group homes began in earnest.

In 1994, the international Salamanca Statement on Principles, Policy and Practice in Special Needs Education (UNESCO, 1994) was produced, supported by over 90 governments, including the UK, and indicating total commitment to inclusive education. *Excellence for all Children* (DfEE, 1997) continued to increase the drive towards inclusion for all, wherein all young people of school age would be educated together in their local schools to enable them to 'flourish in adult life' (ibid: 43)

At the time, however, many parents and professionals were concerned that without adequate training, funding and resources, this drive would be detrimental to some young people in schools as not all teachers had the relevant knowledge to cater for the needs of all children (Wall, 2003). This applies particularly to young people with ASDs whose needs are very specific and were highlighted in the NAS report at that time entitled *Autism – The Invisible Children* (Peacock, et al., 1996) which:

> ...identified the difficulties faced by children and their families as a consequence of poor planning and co-ordination by local authorities and of inadequate support for students with autism in mainstream schools.
>
> (ibid., cited in Barnard et al., 2000: 6)

The report also identified that:

- for those children in preschool and primary settings provision was improving

- fewer improvements were evident in secondary schools

- parents had to work through 'battles' to access diagnoses and provision.

The NAS report of 1999, *Opening the Door*, focused further on these 'battles' as it explored parental issues regarding diagnoses.

With regard to Health, in 1998 the report *A First Class Service* emerged highlighting the government's determination to 'improve the quality of care through continued professional development and professional self-regulation' (Styring and Grant, 2005: 142). This signified the increasing emphasis on quality assurance mechanisms not only to ensure the quality of services but to offer accountability to service users. Yet the involvement of adolescents and adults with learning difficulties (including those with ASDs) in quality procedures was still lacking. This change, however, was beginning to emerge and increasingly throughout the 1990s the voice of the 'consumer' or 'client' in decision-making became increasingly prominent. The change of terminology to 'consumer' or 'client' was also emerging at this time to move away from systems which implied *needs* to those focusing more on individual *rights*.

Until this point in history developments had produced changes in service policy at a steady rate but from the turn of the century in 2000, the speed of change gained pace to such rapidity that it became difficult for many professionals and parents to keep up to date and informed.

In 2000 we saw a major step towards ensuring the quality of care provision. This was through the Care Standards Act (DoH, 2000), the government's response to building on the earlier White Paper entitled *Modernising Social Services:*

The Government recognised that, despite the best efforts of many devoted staff, some social care services were not of a good enough quality, or suited to the needs of the user. There was a need to eliminate inequalities in social care and to provide a system that is convenient to use, responds quickly to emergencies and provides top quality services. There was also a lack of regulation in the care services and it was not clear what standards the public would expect, or staff should meet. (Internet 7)

This major overhaul of care services introduced the National Care Standards Commission (NCSC), the General Social Care Council (GSCC) and improved training for social care workers. From this point on all registered care providers would be subjected to inspections to ensure the National Minimum Standards were being met in a move to increase accountability and raise the quality of services in general. The 2003 Health and Social Care (Community Health and Standards) Act established the Commission for Social Care Inspection (CSCI) which 'incorporates the work done by the Social Services Inspectorate (SSI), the SSI/Audit Commission Joint Review Team and the National Care Standards Commission (NCSC)' (Brammer, 2005: 100), clearly a major step forwards in improving services nationwide as all residential care settings offering levels of personal care have a duty to register with the NCSC. However, there are concerns about levels of ASD knowledge among the staff of such placements and this still exists today. The Harker and King report of 2004 *Tomorrow's Big Problem: Housing Options for People with Autism* echoed this view.

Following the moves towards increased inclusion within education in the 1990s, it had been recognised that effective inclusion does not simply happen by moving young people out of special schools and placing them into mainstream school, and that funding would be needed to ensure effective practices, led by skilled professionals. The NAS report (Barnard et al., 2000), which explored the impact of inclusive educational practices on children, young people and adults with ASDs was quite damning. The overall, and overwhelming, finding of the survey which informed the report was: 'that post-19 there is very little to look forward to' (ibid.: 7). The key findings relating to those over 16 years of age were (ibid.):

- Secondary schools and further education are not meeting the needs of adolescents with autism and Asperger syndrome and parental satisfaction levels decrease the older the child becomes.

- One in five children with an ASD has been excluded from school – nearly twenty times the national average.

- Many adults with ASDs are not included in society at all.

In 2000 the NHS Plan (DoH, 2000b) outlined the targets to be met by the NHS, but rather than affecting the way in which health services were delivered, the targets (which are to be met by 2008) related mostly to health outcomes. To improve accountability for the patients accessing health services the National

Patient Safety Agency (NPSA) was established in 2001 to ensure patient safety when accessing any health provision (Talbot-Smith and Pollock, 2006).

Care trusts were introduced by the NHS Plan of 2000 but the Health and Social Care Act (DoH, 2001) legislated for them. This was a significant step forwards in placing the delivery of health and social care as one aspect of local authority work. Joint funding was encouraged but historical barriers to joint planning, funding and delivery of services resulted in few applications to the Secretary of State for care trust approval. The traditional barriers remain today and fundamental changes of service delivery should be addressed to ensure improved services with more joint working for the most vulnerable people in society.

Valuing People: A New Strategy for Learning Disability in the 21st Century (DoH, 2001b) was seen as a tremendous step forward in improving the lives of people with disabilities, identifying that: 'People with learning disabilities are among the most vulnerable and socially excluded in our society. Very few have jobs, live in their own homes, or have choice over who cares for them' (ibid.: 2). The strategy focuses on all aspects of life for children, young people and adults with learning disabilities in a determined attempt to reduce or even eliminate the inequalities that currently exist:

- Four key areas need to be addressed: rights, independence, choice and inclusion
- Poor planning at point of transition into adulthood
- Insufficient support for carers
- Little or no control over many aspects of their lives
- Health needs are often unmet
- Housing options are limited
- Day services do not always meet individuals' needs
- Limited opportunities for employment
- Needs of those from ethnic minority groups not met
- Inconsistencies in service delivery
- Few examples exist of effective partnerships between health and social care.
  (DoH, 2001b)

The specific difficulties of adolescents and adults with ASDs are acknowledged within the report.

The report offers a useful timeline of targets, target dates and intended outcomes:

- Maximising opportunities for disabled children
- Transition into adult life
- Increased control over own life
- Supporting carers

- Good health
- Housing
- Fulfilling lives
- Employment
- Quality (of services)
- Workforce training
- Partnership working. (ibid.: 26)

If all these objectives can be met then we should begin to see significant changes and progress being made which should lead to enhanced quality of life for all people with learning disabilities. The report itself places a strong emphasis on involving the client group in all major decision-making and the 'expert' advisory teams informing the development of the strategy included a service users' advisory group.

From personal experience I am delighted to see that the caring workforce is to be explored and training implemented, as many of the current workforce across private residential care providers are either unqualified or have limited qualifications. In fact the *Valuing People* report identified that 75 per cent were unqualified (DoH, 2001b: 96). The situation is aggravated by low rates of pay, especially when the responsibilities of the caring roles, with one of the most vulnerable client groups, is considered. As a result, the turnover of staff tends to be high so lack of continuity occurs which significantly affects the behaviour of adults with ASDs.

Improving the quality of services was another of the critical objectives within the *Valuing People* strategy of 2001 which acknowledged that: 'people with autistic spectrum disorders ... have additional and complex needs and achieving good quality services for them requires greater skill and coordination' (DoH, 2001b: 90). Having already acknowledged some of the existing difficulties within the residential care workforce the strategy also made a commitment to inspections of provision and national minimum standards as well as the revision of the social care workforce. A part of the workforce development was the introduction of the Learning Disability Awards Framework (LDAF) which, when fully implemented, will offer all staff access to National Vocational Qualifications (NVQ). Every Learning Disability Partnership Board will be expected to have in place plans for their workforce development and training to ensure implementation is an ongoing part of their planning.

The Special Educational Needs and Disability Discrimination Act (SENDA) (DfES, 2001) changed the face of education considerably with its strong focus on increased inclusion and the right for all children to a mainstream place if their parents wished it. However, there was no guarantee that the school of their choice would either have or offer a place to their child. Following the publication of the Act the Special Educational Needs Code of Practice (DfES, 2001b) was published, guiding teaching staff on how to implement the changes.

Other emphases within the Code of Practice and SENDA included effective parental partnerships, and increased, effective multi-disciplinary working. In Chapter 2, we explored the stages of School Action and School Action Plus which young people with special needs would be placed on according to the levels of difficulty they experienced and for which individual education plans (IEPs) would be devised by the SENCO and class teacher with input from both the parents and the young person themselves.

Shortly after, the government published further guidance for educators including guidance specifically linked to ASDs:

- *Inclusive Schooling: Children with Special Educational Needs* (DfES, 2001c)
- *Special Educational Needs Toolkit* (DfES, 2001d)
- *Autistic Spectrum Disorders: Good Practice Guidance* (DfES/DoH, 2002).

However, concerns arose regarding the amount of legislation and guidance that was emerging and the speed of change with little additional resources being allocated to school budgets to accommodate the changes. Sadly, when very recently undertaking training with educators, I discovered that while 31 of the 40 participants were providing for children or young people with ASDs, not one of them were aware that the ASD guidance even existed. So clearly there appears to be a gap between the government's view on what should be implemented and teachers' knowledge of what is expected. It could be suggested that this guidance may require updating and circulating to everyone working in an education setting with children and adolescents with ASDs.

Relating to adults, negative outcomes were highlighted in the report *Ignored or Ineligible: The Reality for Adults with Autistic Spectrum Disorders* (Barnard et al., 2001) which concluded that:

> Statutory agencies are failing adults with autism or Asperger Syndrome. The majority of individuals and their families are excluded from the care system. They are either ignored or discriminated against through rigid eligibility criteria, often established through ignorance of autism spectrum disorders. In particular, the critical period of transition from adolescents into adulthood is breaking down, and parents are picking up the pieces. (ibid.: 7/8)

In addition other reports (Loynes, 2001a and 2001b) have also identified areas of ASD provision which are falling short of need. In 2002 the NAS published *Autism in Schools: Crisis or Challenge?* (Barnard et al., 2002) highlighting the need for teacher training in ASDs.

So, despite all the changes that have occurred since the 1980s such as increased rights, inclusive practices (within schools and society), parental partnership and multi-disciplinary working there is still evidence which confirms that for many children and young people with ASDs provision in schools is still sadly lacking and does not meet their specific needs. Similarly when adulthood is reached many national systems are still failing many people and their families. So have the changes worked? It would appear there is still a long way to go.

Focusing on provision in care homes the DoH published the *Care Homes for Younger Adults and Adult Placements: National Minimum Standards – Care Home Regulations* (DoH, 2002) which were another outcome of the Care Standards Act of 2000. So now we had a move to ensure improvements in care home provision which sets minimum standards for:

- choice of home

- individual needs and choices

- lifestyle

- personal and healthcare

- complaints procedures

- environment

- staffing

- conduct and management of the home.

The 30 standards include specifically young people and adults with autistic spectrum disorders and recommend that 'individually tailored and comprehensive services' should be developed (DoH, 2002: 3).

In 2002 the Code of Practice for Social Care Workers and Employers was published (Internet 8) to be used as a guide for all those working in the sector who would be assessed by the CSCI during their inspection regime. Set down are clear guidelines regarding acceptable standards of professionalism to be expected within the sector.

The Education Act (DfES, 2002a) gave authority to head teachers to exempt pupils with special needs from taking standard tests. The Qualifications and Curriculum Authority (QCA) offers guidance on the criteria that should be used in such decisions and head teachers should inform parents in writing, along with the governors and the local authority, and parents do have the right to appeal if they feel the decision is inappropriate.

For professionals working with adults with Asperger syndrome the NAS published *Taking Responsibility: Good Practice Guidelines for Services – Adults with Asperger Syndrome* (Powell, 2002). The guidelines cover all aspects of services so are useful to those working in social care, education (secondary schools, FE and HE), housing, employment, Connexions services and health. The guidance was published in acknowledgement of continued problems regarding access to services, lack of community care assessments and exclusion from educational opportunities. The guidelines begin exploring the role of the local authority and make clear recommendations as to how to organise services under the guidance of a senior manager with responsibility for adults with Asperger syndrome. Continuing through a range of issues related to effective provision the guidance offers very constructive and practical suggestions for all professionals.

The next significant legislation to be passed was *Every Child Matters* (DfES, 2003), a strategy which was discussed in Chapter 2 but whose key aim is the:

...greater coordination of human services, such as education, health, social care and youth justice that involves sharing information and working together in new ways to protect children and young people from harm and help them achieve what they want in life. (Florian, 2007: 87)

This was followed in 2005 by *Youth Matters* (DfES, 2006) which was also discussed in Chapter 2. In both the Every Child Matters (ECM) and Youth Matters strategies two of the positive outcomes for young people are emphasised throughout in a desire to eradicate the effects of child poverty and to improve provision for children with disabilities. Along a similar pathway to the significant changes in health and social care services Every Child Matters and Youth Matters set out a national framework of change from central government through local authorities to professionals and parents, with the National Service Framework (NSF) being integral to the developments. The ECM framework of change is further supported by the Children Act (DfES, 2004b) which legislated for some of the key changes, e.g.: directors of children's services, improved inter-agency working systems and practices, integrated inspections, the Children's Commissioner and the review of child protection procedures.

Since the early 1990s more and more young people and adults with learning disabilities (including those with ASDs) have been moving into further or higher education. This was the result of improved knowledge about their needs and more appropriate provision. In 2004 the publication was seen of *Into Higher Education 2004: The Higher Education Guide for People with Disabilities* (SKILL, 2004) which aimed to support students through the transition from school to university studies. SKILL is a national organisation committed to supporting disabled students in HE and this publication clearly guides prospective students through the process from selecting their course to securing a place. Disability support is available and is offered with guidance for students with ASDs included, as well as guidance on Disability Student Allowances which allow students to 'pay for study-related costs that higher education students incur because of their disability' (SKILL, 2004: 31).

In 2003 the focus for social care was on the inspection process through *Fulfilling Lives: Inspection of Social Care Services for People with Learning Disabilities* (Cope, 2003), a response from the previous Valuing People strategy. Exploring the outcomes of a range of inspections conducted between February and November 2001 they were able to draw out key issues that informed the report including: young people with disabilities; transitions, choice and control; supporting carers; health; housing; fulfilling lives; employment; quality services; and partnership working. The inspection teams will focus their attention on seven standards:

1 National Objectives

2 Effectiveness of service delivery and outcomes for users

3 Effectiveness of service delivery and outcomes for carers

4 Quality of services for users and carers – information and care management

5 Social services acting fairly and with consistency

6 Cost and efficiency of services

7 Organisation and management structure.

In 2003 *Independence Matters: An Overview of the Performance of Social Care Services for Physically and Sensory Disabled People.* (Clark, 2003) was published, bringing together the findings of inspections during 2002–3. While the report acknowledged that some positive changes had occurred since the revised government agenda it also showed that a lot more needs to be done to remove barriers to equal opportunities for all people. Categorised into four 'key themes' these areas are:

• Independence at home

• Identity and belonging

• Active citizenship

• Systems and processes. (Clark, 2003: 5/6)

For people with learning disabilities the key themes are:

• Helping people to live more independently

• Creating fairer, more consistent services

• Making services fit individual need

• Improving joint working between health and social care. (ibid.: 8)

Within the field of education the Audit Commission published their findings of a review of SEN provision in 2002. *Special Educational Needs: A Mainstream Issue* explored the progress of authorities and settings in managing and providing quality services for children with SEN and concluded that: '... some [children] continue to face considerable barriers to learning ...' (2002: 51) The report made ten recommendations for improvement.

In 2004, *Removing Barriers to Achievement – The Government Strategy for Special Needs* (RBA) was published (DfES, 2004c) taking into account many of the recommendations of the Audit Commission's report. The RBA strategy outlined the government's vision for continued improvements in SEN provision. Chapters focused on: Early identification, removing barriers to learning, raising expectations and achievements, delivering improved partnerships and interagency working. We also saw the establishment of a team of National SEN Advisers in 2004 to work with local authorities on ways forward.

Early in 2005 the government published *Improving the Life Chances of Disabled People*, with the ambitious aim that: 'By 2025, disabled people in Britain should have full opportunities and choices to improve their quality of life and will be respected and included as equal members of society' (Internet 9). Of the four key areas identified one relates specifically to families with children with disabilities, ensuring that provision is tailor-made to respond to individual child and family needs and that parents should have access to their own individualised budgets offering them greater choice and control over their provision. This links directly to the government's Direct Payments Scheme (DoH, 2004b) which offers parents of disabled children (aged 0–17 years) the option of receiving direct payments from the government to arrange their own package of services to respond to their child's needs. Adults with learning disabilities can also apply for their own Direct Payments so they can devise their own care packages.

The Learning Disability Task Force (LDTF) was established from the Valuing People strategy in 2001 and included significant involvement of people with learning disabilities. In 2004 the Task Force published their report *Rights, Independence, Choice and Inclusion* (LDTF, 2004) which identified the significant changes that had been taking place but also highlighted major changes that were still needed:

> The Task Force believes that people with learning disabilities are still being excluded and discriminated against by services and society. This means that people with learning disabilities are still getting treated unfairly and missing out on the things that other people get. ... The Task Force wants urgent action to be taken to support and include these people and their families.　　(LDTF, 2004: 13)

So since the turn of this century we have begun to see a deluge of legislation, government strategies, guidance documents and reports which all focus on the key areas needed for change. One of the key changes is that of joint working across departments and agencies to provide more of a 'seamless' service for all service users. This could mean that any parent of a child with an ASD or an adult with an ASD could have one 'lead professional' who works with professionals from other agencies so information can be shared more easily. However, we are still seeing the publication of separate DoH and DfES documents which presents a contradiction between the government's philosophy of joint working and their recommendations.

In 2004 Ofsted published *Special Educational Needs and Disability: Towards Inclusive Schools* (Ofsted, 2004d) which explored ways in which schools were increasing their inclusive practices since the inclusion agenda began. They found that while some evidence of good practice was evident there were still major areas of concern such as '... inaccessible premises and shortfalls in support to reach their potential' (ibid.: 23).

On the progressive theme of improving health and social care the *National Standards. Local Action: Health and Social Care Standards and Planning Framework* (DoH, 2004c) included all the standards to be met by health and social care professionals by which providers will be inspected by the CSCI. However, some have voiced concerns as to whether inspections will be nothing more than an assessment against a checklist of standards (Styring and Grant, 2005). The NAS offers guidance for inspectors working for the NCSC on their website ensuring they are well informed of the specific needs of service users with ASDs.

In a different area completely 2004 saw the arrival of the Mental Capacity Bill which '... provides a comprehensive legal framework for decision-making on behalf of those who lack capacity' (Brammer, 2005: 95). This could be useful for those adults with ASDs who have no means of communicating, although it would be hoped that in time the numbers who cannot communicate in any way will diminish through improved practices.

Staying with health, 2004 saw the emergence of the NHS Improvement Plan (DoH, 2004d) outlining a planning framework in which PCTs will identify the needs of their patient base and account for them in their Local Delivery Plans. In addition they will continue to commission services (primary health services, secondary health services and specialist services). However, there are further plans that move to GPs commissioning their own services directly.

The Disability Rights Task Force identified key barriers to improving services for disabled people in their 1999 report *From Exclusion to Inclusion* (Disability Rights Task Force, 1999). In 2004 the Department of Work and Pensions (DWP) published the findings of a study which explored these key barriers, entitled: *Making Transitions: Addressing barriers in services for disabled people* (Internet 11). The report focused specifically on periods of transition as previous findings suggested that it was at these times that the greatest problems occurred: Transitions from child to adult services, between educational settings, into and between employment, moving from one local authority to another and between different situations such as home, hospital and other forms of accommodation (Internet 10). The main issues discovered were the barriers preventing access to services at transition points and/or delays in securing those services, such as:

- organisational structures (poor liaison and joint working, flexibility, etc.)
- budget boundaries and budget regulations impacting on the availability of funding needed to secure services
- procedural issues (access to relevant information about local services, missing information, poor transition planning, etc.).

Several reports have highlighted the increase in mental health problems in adulthood among adults with ASDs. The Mental Capacity Act (DoH, 2005) is particularly pertinent and will be implemented in 2007. By means of the Act the Independent Mental Advocate Service is established which '... aims to help particularly vulnerable people who lack capacity who are facing important decisions made by the NHS and local authorities' (Internet 11).

The Education Act (DfES, 2005a) introduced the School Profile which will replace the annual governing body's report with a broader-ranging document which will be posted on a national website to enable open access. The Education Act legislated for *The Framework for the Inspection of Schools* (Ofsted, 2005) which revised existing inspection processes, the main areas for inspection being:

- Quality of education provided by schools
- Educational standards achieved in those schools
- Quality of leadership in and management of those schools
- Spiritual, moral, social and cultural development of pupils at these schools
- Extent to which the education provided by schools meets the needs of the range of pupils
- Contribution made by schools in England to the well-being of their pupils.

(Florian, 2007: 88)

Inspections take place on a three-yearly cycle and little notice is now given before the inspection is due to begin. Special educational needs provision is an integral part of the inspection process and parents are entitled to contribute to that process. The findings of the inspection are laid out in report form and all inspection reports are published on the Ofsted website. This gives parents access to school inspection reports which may help to inform their decisions about the choice of school for their children.

In 2005 the government produced their *Annual Report on Learning Disability. Valuing People: Making Things Better* (HM Government, 2005b) which provided an update on the progress made since the introduction of the Valuing People strategy across all aspects of all services. The report identified the key areas of focus during the previous year and worked closely with the National Forum for People with Learning Disabilities, the Valuing People team and the Learning Disability Task Force. The four areas were:

- People with high support needs
- Community safety
- Family carers
- Stopping people being sent to live away from their communities.

(HM Government, 2005b: 14)

The report concluded that while significant improvements have been made there was still a considerable amount of more work to be done in future years.

The Disability Discrimination Act of 1995 has been updated by the Disability Discrimination Act of 2005, predominantly to ensure increased equality for all people with disabilities. The Disability Rights Commission has also published the Disability Discrimination Codes of Practice including a version relating to over-16s in education (Internet 12). The detail included in this Code of Practice is thorough and for those not familiar with all the requirements on education providers in FE and HE the Code is a useful reference tool. Guidance relates to the following areas:

- Understanding the social dimension of disability
- Recognising the diverse nature of disability

- Avoiding making assumptions
- Finding out about disabled people's requirements
- Seeking expert advice
- Planning ahead
- Auditing policies and procedures
- Implementing anti-discriminatory policies and practices
- Gathering information
- Attracting disabled applicants
- Promoting a positive image
- Resolving disputes. (Internet 12)

In 2006 a White Paper *Our Health, Our Care, Our Say: A new direction for Community Services* (Internet 7) was published which included several areas relating to the health and social care of those with learning disabilities: shifting expenditure from hospitals to the community, bringing some health specialisms into local communities, encouraging local community hospitals, providing Personal Health and Social Care Plans, more support for carers and the extension of direct payments, and the piloting of individual budgets for social care (Internet 13). If such proposals were to be implemented it should follow that access to services would be made easier for those with ASDs.

June 2006 saw the publication of *Introducing the Office for Disability Issues* (HM Government, 2006) outlining the roles and responsibilities of this newly formed government office. The Office:

...aims to make sure that:

- the Government takes action to support disabled people and improve their quality of life
- disabled people's needs and views are at the centre of the Government's work on disability, and
- disabled people are respected as equal members of society. (ibid.: 3)

In 2006 the National Forum for Organisations of Disabled People was renamed Equality 2025 – the United Kingdom Advisory Network on Disability Equality, to be referred to as Equality 2025 (Internet 14). The aim of this newly formed group was to ensure that the recommendations from *Improving Life Chances of Disabled People* (Internet 9) were translated into effective practice through the involvement of people with disabilities in decision-making processes at national level. This is in support of the government's aim for full equality for all people with learning disabilities by 2025.

July 2006 saw the publication of the House of Commons Education and Skills Committee report: *Special Educational Needs: Third Report of Sessions 2005–6,*

Volume One (House of Commons, 2006). This report was informed by 230 communications and concluded that many parents and their children with special educational needs are still being failed by current SEN policies and practices – a damning statement. The report strongly recommends considerable investment in training the education workforce to improve knowledge, understanding and thus, provision. Overall the report concludes that parental partnerships, provision in schools, the statementing process, training for staff, inclusion and budgets are all areas needing considerable overhaul. It also highlights the long-term cost effectiveness of appropriate provision that will help improve outcomes for all adults with learning disabilities. While the government shows no indication of reviewing SEN provision the report highlights a range of areas whereby the current system is failing and states that it is simply unacceptable that the government refuses to initiate a national review. The 2002 Audit Commission report suggested such a review, yet now, in 2007, there are still no positive moves in this direction.

While much of the preceding legislation and guidance has related to learning disability it would, by definition, include provision for young people and adults with ASDs. It has also been necessary to consider documents relating to children as the appropriateness of provision for younger children impacts on later provision and outcomes in adulthood. If we can ensure all children's needs can be met up to the age of 16 then it should follow that needs can be met after 16 and into adulthood.

The DoH published guidance on *Better Services for People with Autistic Spectrum Disorders* in 2006. This is one of the few documents relating specifically to ASDs and the fact that it took till 2006 to produce the guidance reflects on the lack of understanding that people with ASDs have very specific needs that cannot generally be met through generic learning disability policies. The report states that while some people with ASDs receive appropriate provision, for the remainder this is not the case. Referring to all previous government initiatives the report makes it clear that for people with ASDs we need to ensure that all professionals have adequate understanding of the characteristics and effects of ASDs and how to provide appropriate opportunities to ensure individuals are working towards their maximum potential. The report goes on to outline key ways forward:

- Joint working systems should ensure the needs of people with ASDs can be met quickly and within their local community.
- Social inclusion must be developed.
- Care assessment plans must be in place for all people with ASDs.
- Direct payments and individualised budgets may help people with ASDs.
- People with ASDs must have a say in their provision.
- Advocacy support should be made available for those who need it.
- Respite care should be more readily available.

- Carers should be better supported.
- Staff training is needed.
- Employment opportunities should be considered for those who wish to be employed.
- Diagnoses should be more readily available.
- Health plans should be in place for those who need it.
- A range of housing options need to be available.
- Changes in provision should be carefully planned.

As can be seen the recommendations are far reaching and, arguably, long overdue, but if they can be turned into reality then hopefully we will begin to see more successes in the future.

Also in 2006 the DRC published *Changing Britain for good. Putting Disability at the Heart of Public Policy* (Internet 12). Following extensive consultation the report states that:

> In reality, as the DRC's Disability Debate, launched in June 2005, has established, Britain's main public policy goals – economic prosperity, full employment, an end to child poverty, better health, less crime – will fail unless the experiences of people with impairments and long term health conditions are acknowledged and addressed. (Internet 12)

The report goes on to identify ten goals to be achieved for increased fulfilment of the lives of people with disabilities and for increased equality.

Rob Greig, the National Director of the Valuing People strategy, published *Values and Visions: Services for People with a Learning Disability* (Greig, 2006) in which he highlights the positive changes that have occurred and the priorities for 2006/7. Examples of positive changes included:

- healthcare commission giving high priority to the needs of those with learning disabilities
- national policy now incorporating disability group
- increases in independent living
- person-centred planning being established more
- carers groups increase.

However, Greig goes on to clarify the key priorities for 2006/7 including an increase in local services for service users, resolving funding issues and increased employment opportunities for all service users.

Employment issues were the focus of the DWP report *Improving Work Opportunities for People with a Learning Disability* (DWP, 2006) whose remit was:

> ... to identify the barriers facing people with learning disabilities entering employment and to make recommendations for overcoming those barriers, thus increasing the numbers entering paid work wherever possible. (ibid.: 1)

This detailed report uses case studies to indicate the potential many people with learning disabilities have and the positive impact they can have on a workplace, to say nothing of the positive impact employment can have on the individual with a learning disability. Again, as is becoming accepted practice, people with learning disabilities were included in the working group responsible for informing the report. The report identified nine key messages that informed the report, including the fact that people with learning disabilities are people and active citizens first, person-centred planning is essential, transition planning is needed and budgetary resources are needed to support future developments in the area. The report went on to make 42 significant recommendations starting with developments in secondary schools, FE and HE to develop work potential and forge links with future employers, then going on to identify the barriers in the field of work and suggestions for improvements. This is, in my view, a key document for progress but will depend on the attitudes and support from society as a whole and employers and their employees in particular.

A thought on human rights and disability rights

One of the early – and significant – human rights statements relating to learning disability and mental health was the United Nations Declaration on the Rights of Mentally Retarded People (1971) which clarified rights relating to education, citizenship, health and work (Richardson, 2005: 80). Yet over 30 years since its publication we are still campaigning for the same issues – is this the outcome of a positive and inclusive society?

Back in 1992, at the 4th Autism-Europe Congress, the European Charter for Persons with Autism was passed, which was later adopted by the European Parliament in 1996. While acknowledging previous human rights the Charter identified 19 rights specific to people with ASDs relating to all aspects of living in an included society. Areas covered include: housing, employment, education, support, appropriate services, choice and inclusion.

The Human Rights Act of 1998 (HMSO, 1998) supported 'best practice' for all people with learning disabilities and offered those who felt they had been unfairly treated an opportunity to challenge decisions legally. The Mental Capacity Act of 2005 should further support those who are not able to make personal representation.

These two examples of human rights developments, along with other discrimination legislation highlighted in this chapter, support the rights of all people, and wider society needs to accept and include people with learning disabilities (including those with ASDs) more. However, it could be argued the frustration is that many of the issues we are currently campaigning for are the same issues we were fighting for 20 or 30 years ago, so how much progress has been made? The Disability Rights Commission (Internet 12) offers a wealth of information relating to disability rights and practical guidance documents for all aspects of services relating to learning disability.

Regarding people with ASDs, Broach et al.'s report *Autism: Rights in Reality* (2003) presented a very negative picture of the situation at the time:

> People with autistic spectrum disorders and their families are not getting the help they need. This is despite increased recognition of these disorders which are thought to affect 1 in every 100 people. However, autism and Asperger syndrome do not fit the current ways of thinking about disability and the existing criteria for eligibility for many services. A lack of professional understanding and contradictory or confusing guidance from central government mean that support services for children and adults with disabilities continue to be designed without autism in mind. (Broach et al., 2003: 1)

Focusing on seven areas of everyday life – social care, finances, transport, leisure, housing, carers support and advocacy – the report surveyed the members of the NAS and found services were still not meeting needs. The report concluded with recommendations for change across each of the seven areas involving 'minimal costs for a substantial gain in terms of social inclusion for people with autistic spectrum disorders' (Broach et al., 2003: 29).

Summary

We have seen that the amount of legislation, guidance and reports relating to learning disability, ASDs and rights is immense. The documents covered in this chronology demonstrate that key issues have emerged again and again over 20 or 30 years yet we are still campaigning for further developments on each of these issues. This raises significant questions regarding progress. In addition we have explored the need for increased joint working across professional boundaries yet at the national level we are still seeing the emergence of information from separate departments and organisations, each with their own perspective. At the local level we now have Learning Disability Partnership Boards which are representative of all agencies and groups involved with the client group, so why at the national level do we still have the DoH and DfES working independently? Arguably messages are confusing and contradictory.

Reports and guidance that have been published tend to highlight the same issues but are professionals and carers supposed to have knowledge of all these? This is an unreasonable expectation as professionals and carers lives are often frantic enough simply completing their daily tasks. If carers and individuals have to fight for their entitlements this is demanding and stressful, just as daily working for professionals in the field is likely to be demanding and stressful. However, if professionals are not aware of the potential outcomes for adults with ASDs if provision is not effective, do not have a thorough understanding of ASDs and have not accessed the practical guidance documents on effective provision then how can we expect change? Within the field we have seen considerable progress over the years but significant changes in policy and practice must occur to ensure positive changes continue resulting in greater inclusion for all adults with ASDs within their own society and communities.

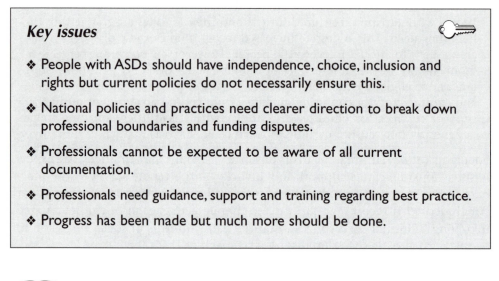

Key issues

❖ People with ASDs should have independence, choice, inclusion and rights but current policies do not necessarily ensure this.

❖ National policies and practices need clearer direction to break down professional boundaries and funding disputes.

❖ Professionals cannot be expected to be aware of all current documentation.

❖ Professionals need guidance, support and training regarding best practice.

❖ Progress has been made but much more should be done.

Suggested further reading

Barnard, J., Harvey, V., Potter, D. and Prior, A. (2001) *Ignored or Ineligible? The Reality for Adults with Autism Spectrum Disorders.* London: NAS.

Barnard, J., Broach, S., Potter, D. and Prior, A. (2002) *Autism in Schools: Crisis or Challenge?* London: NAS.

Broach, S., Camgöz, S., Heather, C., Owen, G., Potter, D. and Prior, A. (2003) *Autism: Rights in Reality.* London: NAS.

APPENDIX: TIMELINE OF SIGNIFICANT LEGISLATION, REPORTS AND GUIDANCE

Health and/or social care related	Date	Education related	Date	Rights related	Date	ASD related	Date
Poor Law commission set up	1833		1833		1833		1833
Poor Law Amendments Act	1845		1845		1845		1845
Lunacy Act/Insanity Act	1845		1845		1845		1845
Lunatic Asylums Act	1853		1853		1853		1853
Lunatics Amendment Act	1862		1862		1862		1862
	1870	Forster's Education Act	1870		1870		1870
Idiots Act	1881		1881		1881		1881
	1909	Education Act	1909		1909		1909
Mental Deficiency Act	1913		1913		1913		1913
Beveridge Report	1942		1942		1942		1942
	1944	Education Act	1944		1944		1944
	1945	Handicapped Pupils and School Health Regulations	1945		1945		1945
Advent of National Health Service	1948		1948		1948		1948
	1962		1962		1962	National Autistic Society formed	1962
	1970	Education (Handicapped Children) Act	1970				
	1970						

© Education and Care for Adolescents and Adults with Autism, Sage 2007 © Kate Wall

Health and/or social care related	Date	Education related	Date	Rights related	Date	ASD related
White Paper: *Better Services for the Mentally Handicapped*	1971		1971	UN Convention on the Rights of Mentally Retarded Persons	1971	
	1976	Court Report	1976		1976	
	1978	Warnock Report	1978		1978	
	1981	Education Act	1981		1981	
Mental Health Act	1983		1983		1983	
Making a Reality of Community Care report	1986		1986		1986	
Community Care: Agenda for action initiative	1988		1988		1988	
Caring for People initiative Children Act	1989		1989		1989	
National Health Services and Community Care Act	1990	Education Act	1990		1990	
	1993	SEN Code of Practice	1993		1993	
	1994	Salamanca Statement on Principles, Policy and Practice in Special Needs Education	1994		1994	
	1995		1995	Disability Discrimination Act	1995	

Health and/or social care related	Date	Education related	Date	Rights related	Date	ASD related
	1996	Nursery Education and Maintained Schools Act	1996		1996	Report: Autism – The Invisible Children
White Paper: *The New NHS. Modern, Dependable*	1997	Excellence for All	1997		1997	
A First Class Service report; White Paper: *Modernising Social Services*	1998		1998	Human Rights Act	1998	
	1999		1999	Report: *From Exclusion to Inclusion*	1999	Report: *Opening the Door*
NHS Plan introduced; Care Standards Act	2000		2000		2000	
National Patient Safety Agency established; Valuing People: A New Strategy for Learning Disability in the 21st Century; Heath and Social Care Act	2001	Special Educational Needs and Disability Discrimination Act; Guidance document: *Inclusive Schooling: Children with SEN*; SEN Toolkit published	2001	Special Educational Needs and Disability Discrimination Act	2001	Report: *Ignored or Ineligible: The Reality for Adults with Autistic Spectrum Disorders*

Health and/or social care related	Date	Education related	Date	Rights related	Date	ASD related
Care Homes for Younger Adults and Adult Placements: National Minimum Standards – Care Home Regulations	2002	Educational guidance document published: *ASDs: Good Practice Guidance*	2002		2002	Educational guidance document published: *ASDs: Good Practice Guidance*
Code of Practice for Social Care Workers and Employers		*Special Educational Needs: A Mainstream Issue*				*Report: Autism in Schools: Crisis or Challenge?*
Fair Access to Care Services: guideance on eligibility criteria for adult social care		Education Act				*Guidance: Taking Responsibility: Good Practice Guidelines for Services – Adults with Asperger Syndrome*
Every Child Matters	2003	*Every Child Matters*	2003	*Every Child Matters*	2003	
Fulfilling Lives: Inspection of Services for People with Learning Disabilities Health & Social Care (Community & Standards) Act						

Health and/or social care related	Date	Education related	Date	Rights related	Date	ASD related
Independence Matters: An overview of the performance of social care service for physically and sensory disabled people Children Act	2004	Children Act	2004	Rights, independence, choice and inclusion	2004	Report: *Tomorrow's Big Problem: Housing Options for People with Autism*
Direct Payments scheme introduced National Standards: Local – Action – Health and Social Care Standards and Planning Framework Mental Capacity Bill		Into Higher Education 2004: The higher education guide for people with disabilities National SEN Advisers established Special Educational Needs and Disability: Towards Inclusive Schools				
NHS Improvement Plan Youth Matters Improving the Life Chances of Disabled People	2005	Youth Matters SEN and Disability Discrimination Act	2005	Youth Matters	2005	

© Education and Care for Adolescents and Adults with Autism, Sage 2007 © Kate Wall

Health and/or social care related	Date	Education related	Date	Rights related	Date	ASD related
Health and Social Care Information Centre		Education Act (incorporating Revised Framework for the Inspection of Schools) Education and Skills White Paper				
Mental Capacity Act						
White Paper: *Our Health, Our Care, Our Say: A New Direction for Community Services*	2006	House of Commons report: *SEN: Third Report of Sessions 2005–6*	2006	Equality 2025 – The UK Advisory Network on Disability Equality established	2006	Better Services for People with Autistic Spectrum Disorders
Introducing the Office for Disability						
Better Services for People Autistic Spectrum Disorders						
Values and Visions: Services for People with a Learning Disability						
Improving Work Opportunities for People with a Learning Disability						

4

Understanding the world of autism

This chapter explores:
➤ the key features of ASDs;
➤ effects of ASDs on individuals;
➤ the individuality of ASDs;
➤ implications for practice.

Introduction

To be able to provide successfully for adolescents and adults with autism we need to have our own theoretical and working knowledge and understanding of ASDs. We cannot assume to be able to understand the difficulties people with autism are experiencing if we do not have basic knowledge of this complex disorder. Without this our attempts to provide appropriately for those we work with are likely to be unsuccessful or futile, and if we are not careful, may actually compound their difficulties even further.

If a young man, Peter, always gets up, showers and dresses in the same order, has to have a Frank Sinatra tape playing at the time and will not open the curtains until the end of track 7, then so be it. No harm is being done to anyone and the required tasks are completed. However, if this scenario changes slightly we could have a very different outcome. In a residential care home staff illness may mean that bank staff are called in to provide cover. A member of the bank staff, who does not know Peter, may decide to wake him and draw the curtains to encourage him to get up and have a shower. Result – an outburst of very difficult behaviour. Simply through ensuring that all staff (including temporary staff) have autism–specific knowledge and are aware of the individual characteristics of each resident, this scenario could have been avoided, the behavioural outburst would not have occurred and Peter's routine maintained.

Throughout this chapter we will unravel the world of autism to offer increased understanding to parents and professionals alike. Having already explored the triad of impairments in Chapter 2 we will continue to look in more detail at each of the areas of difficulty experienced by people with ASDs, which should cast some light and clarification on some of the behaviours we have become familiar with in our work but may not have appreciated fully. With this knowledge we will be in a far better position to understand more of the behaviours of people with ASDs and thus our working practices should be enhanced, offering increased and more appropriate opportunities to the adults and hopefully enabling them to work towards their full potential.

The individuality of ASDs

What should always be remembered is that like every human being, people with ASDs are individual and unique. There is not one blanket description for all autistic spectrum difficulties which every person diagnosed with an ASD will experience. Each person will have been, and will continue to be affected, by their own unique likes and dislikes, preferred activities, strengths and weaknesses, current levels of competence and the environments they find themselves in. Whether in the home, school, college, health setting or residential care setting we, as professionals, should take each of these into account in our work and/or caring roles.

Each individual with autism will have progressed along their own developmental path at their own rate, and unless we have knowledge of their history and identify their individual levels of current competence in each of the key areas of difficulty, we are unlikely to be able to offer useful and appropriate activities that are likely to encourage and sustain continued progress.

One important area to reflect on is that of the more able adult with an ASD whose abilities can often mask the areas of real difficulty they experience. Anyone who has heard Ros Blackburn, Wendy Lawson or Temple Grandin speak about their views of the world as adults with ASDs will see and hear coherent, fluent and confident speakers capable of entertaining an audience of several hundred, with excellent abilities to clearly explain their life experiences. Yet fluency and confidence can mask their inability to complete simple and basic tasks such as making a sandwich. Ros considers her ability to be her greatest disability as people assume her abilities are consistent across all skill areas. Sadly, the outcomes of being misunderstood are significant and for the undiagnosed the outcomes can be compounded yet further, as Jordan (1999) suggests:

> Undiagnosed pupils often end in schools for children with emotional and behavioural difficulties, which (unless the school has made special provision) are unlikely to be suitable. Undiagnosed adults with autism may end up on the streets or even in prison because their behaviour is misunderstood and they are vulnerable to manipulation by others. (p. 115)

I would extend this view beyond the undiagnosed as even those with a diagnosis can still be misunderstood and 'manipulated', and if inappropriate provision is offered, this can result in similar and often negative outcomes. If we are not careful our lack of autism-specific knowledge can encourage us to focus strongly on the behaviour outbursts that can readily occur and our attentions and focus may then concentrate on modifying the undesirable behaviours. Conversely if we reflected on the reasons for the outbursts and could identify links between the antecedents and the person's ASD difficulties, we may be able to make changes that would result in a reduction or elimination of the behaviour outbursts. Until we can be assured that all professionals working with adolescents and adults with autism have acceptable levels of knowledge and understanding of ASDs then we cannot assume things will change.

In developing our understanding of the individuality of adults with ASDs we need to consider the person first and the autism second, which can only be achieved by reflecting on their developmental history, educational history and current strengths and weaknesses and then moving on to add our own knowledge of ASDs to help offer explanations and inform our planning. As previously mentioned there may well be an imbalance between individual abilities and difficulties so we should remain open minded and not assume that if an individual is a competent communicator they will be competent in all areas. Ros Blackburn, Wendy Lawson and Temple Grandin all emphasise the fact that they are able to speak publicly as they are in control, they know the audience will behave in a certain way (politely) and they are unlikely to face any unexpected events during their delivery. Their difficulties in other areas will not be obvious or be tested in any way.

Key areas of difficulty

Referring back to the triad of impairments from Chapter 2 we are reminded of the three key areas of difficulty experienced by individuals with ASDs:

- social interaction
- social communication
- imagination.

These difficulties are often accompanied by unusual, repetitive and stereotypical behaviours. As discussed earlier in this chapter each individual will demonstrate their difficulties at their own level of severity from mild to severe, but difficulties in each area will be present. Whitman (2004: 52) offers 'the general characteristics' of autism:

1 Sensory processing problems

2 Motor dysfunctions

3 Arousal/activation problems

4 Cognitive deficiencies

5 Social interaction problems

6 Language deficiencies

7 Repetitive, restricted and stereotyped interests, activities and behaviours (self-regulation)

8 Behaviour problems

9 Physical/medical features.

Prior to reaching adolescence or adulthood the individual will also have experienced many adults, all of whom would have been trying to help them with their difficulties. However, this group of albeit well intentioned people, through their lack of knowledge, may have compounded the difficulties of the individual, so as professionals we must be prepared for welcoming some individuals who will appear extremely difficult to manage and to support appropriately. A detailed history will support our work.

Expanding further on the three areas within the triad of impairments we can clarify typical characteristics of an ASD as follows.

- Social interaction:

    - avoids eye contact
    - lacks desire to interact or play with children or adults
    - appears oblivious to the world around
    - is not interested in being talked to or played with or having physical contact
    - lack of cooperative play
    - lack of desire to establish relationships and friendships
    - unable to interpret or understand peoples feelings and emotions
    - does not respond to affection or being touched or appears to overreact to these.

- Social communication (speech, language and non-verbal communication):

    - lack of useful language
    - lack of desire to communicate with others around them
    - echolalia
    - inability to understand non-verbal communication such as gestures and facial expression
    - inability to understand the process of conversation
    - if speech develops, it will be delayed and may demonstrate unusual speech, unusual or monotonous tone and/or patterns of speech
    - may talk about a topic incessantly and at inappropriate times
    - may be able to use language appropriately in one situation but be unable to transfer the language into an alternative situation.

- Imagination:
  - – lack of imaginative play when growing up
  - – activities may be rigid, stereotypical and repetitive
  - – resistance to participation in imaginative situations
  - – repetitive and/or obsessive behaviours
  - – difficulties and anxieties coping with unexpected change.

In addition to the characteristics above the following may be observed:

- repetitive movements such as hand flapping, rocking, toe walking or covering ears or eyes
- unusual response to stimuli. Individuals with autism may be over-or-under sensitive to some sensory stimuli. Examples would include: refusal to eat 'lumpy' food or combined foods such as sandwiches; aversion to common noises such as a dishwasher or vacuum cleaner; apparent lack of awareness of cold, heat and general dangers (this raises particular issues of possible danger)
- difficulties with poor or delayed motor coordination – gross body and/or fine/motor
- unusual responses to 'normal' situations
- self-harming or inappropriate behaviour, such as over–aggression
- erratic sleeping patterns
- a skill that the adult excels at – usually in art, knowledge of a specific subject, music or mathematics. Adults with such an exceptional skill are known as 'autistic savants'.

Case Study 4.1 Peter in secondary school

Peter has Asperger syndrome and has just entered Year 10 at secondary school and is commencing his GCSE study programmes in ten subjects. He retains several subject teachers but faces many changes, including meeting Mr Phelps the history teacher. The lessons are now much more focused but there are also more groupwork exercises to work on with his peers. Mr Phelps is a demanding teacher who does not appear to have much patience. He is known for shouting at any member of the class who is not on task and picks out students to give answers to questions. Peter has sensory difficulties with his hearing as he does not register louder noises but can often pick up on much quieter sounds from within and outside of the classroom which others cannot hear. Peter finds this very distracting. In addition he can be easily distracted by bright displays in classrooms and works well in a distraction-free environment. Peter's biggest problem has always been social interactions with others (peers and teachers). He has always been perceived by his peers as a bit of an outsider who behaves oddly at times. He is not known for his interest in typical teenage boy distractions but is a genius working on the computer, where he spends as much time as possible.

Think about the following:

1 Why do you think Peter chooses to spend time on the computer?

2 What difficulties might Mr Phelps create for Peter?

3 What changes could be made to the classroom environment to accommodate Peter's difficulties?

4 How well do you think Peter will cope with groupwork?

Identify the reasons for your answers.

Case study 4.2: Martin in a residential setting

Martin is 25 and has just entered a private residential care home for adults with learning disabilities. He is the only resident with an ASD and has particular difficulties with changes. He does not attempt to establish relationships with others and insists on having his own space, the same place in the dining room and the same cutlery and crockery. When distressed he is prone to outbursts of violent behaviour and/or self-harming. He is assigned a key worker, Emily, who encourages him by patting him on the back. She talks to him and insists he looks at her when she addresses him and that he does not walk away when she is speaking to him. Emily is working on his social skills through seating him on a table with three other residents at meal times and sitting him in the lounge during the evenings with the other residents to watch one hour's television with his housemates. Both of these incidences result in outbursts of inappropriate behaviour which are dealt with by giving him time out in another room.

Think about the following:

1 Why do you think Martin reacts negatively to the dining room placement?

2 How could Emily change her approach to respond more directly to Martin's needs?

3 Is time out an appropriate response to Martin's behaviour outbursts?

Identify the reasons for your answers

Through discussing each area of difficulty highlighted above we will be able to increase our levels of understanding.

Social interaction

Throughout childhood we generally observe children who establish relationships with the key people in their lives from a very early age. If we think of the baby who recognises his/her mother's voice and begins to squirm and wriggle in anticipation we can imagine the origins of our social interactions. For adolescents and adults with ASDs this basic level of interaction may not have happened at all or may have appeared in their infancy but then disappeared a few years later. In its simplest form these adults do not feel the need to interact with others as they find this difficult to manage and understand and at times find very threatening or confusing. Therefore it is simpler to avoid such situations. So in the case studies Peter could find the group work particularly difficult and Martin would find being forced to respond to Emily's conversations very difficult to deal with – hence the outbursts of inappropriate behaviours. Neither Peter nor Martin intend to be rude, they simply prefer to avoid such situations and may demonstrate unusual behaviours in such situations.

This lack of desire to interact with others will have significantly affected the social development of the individual and is likely to have resulted in lack of friendships. For adolescents, friendships are usually extremely important so this difference is likely to have made the individual appear aloof, odd or indifferent and other adolescents are likely to simply avoid contact with them or, sadly, pick on them. The result is the adolescent can become socially isolated, which then makes further social interactions even more unlikely. While many adolescents will be phoning or texting their friends to make arrangements for their next evening out the adolescent with ASD will be more solitary and happy with their own company. For families this can be a difficult situation as it will affect the socialisation of the whole family. If the adolescent is distressed by being around people who may not really understand his/her ASD then attending barbecues and parties with family friends can be very difficult. In turn the ASD has a considerable effect on each and every family member. Imagine the annual family holiday – to a new venue, meeting new people and visiting unfamiliar places. For the adolescent or adult with an ASD this can be incredibly stressful and it may be decided by the family that the difficulties it raises and the stress of coping with those difficulties renders it impossible. Other family events such as Christmas and birthdays may be just as problematic.

Social interaction is generally developed through eye contact between two people and this again is an area which is likely to be very difficult for adolescents and adults with ASDs. If sharing eye contact means the other person may place expectations on you to engage in an activity you are unsure about, or to engage in a conversation, it is much easier to avoid eye contact in the first place to avoid confusion. To compensate it is common for individuals with ASDs to use peripheral vision to observe or look at other people. From looking out of the corner of the eye we are not placing ourselves in such a vulnerable position but are still able to engage in a comfortable level of interaction. Therefore to insist on eye contact can be distressing, but to encourage eye contact could be a positive move forwards with some individuals.

For adolescents and adults who are meeting people for the first time it is customary to shake hands or to share a kiss on the cheek. If you have an ASD and are very sensitive to touch, a simple handshake may feel very painful, so again it is easier to avoid such situations, despite others perhaps considering you rude if you ignore the offered hand and turn away.

An additional problem for individuals with ASDs is their inability to understand, interpret and use emotions and feelings in acceptable ways. An adult with an ASD may hit out at another resident frequently and enjoy the sound of their crying, not able to appreciate the fact that they have hurt that person. The crying rewards the behaviour and therefore it is likely to be repeated.

What is important to remember at this point is that those professionals who are familiar with the characteristics of ASDs will have devised strategies which directly respond to the individual needs of the people with ASD they have worked with. They will also be familiar with a system of working practice that involves observations and detailed planning to ensure appropriate activities are offered to encourage progress and success.

Social communication

Some adolescents and adults with ASDs will not develop useful speech throughout their lives, some will master a signing system to be used in place of speech and some will be fluent speakers. However, being a fluent speaker is not the same as being a fluent communicator as the process of communication involves two-way (or more) conversation and conversation involves rules that often elude individuals with ASDs. Wendy Lawson, Ros Blackburn and Temple Grandin are excellent examples of fluent speakers and I was fortunate to talk with Temple at a conference. After some stilted conversation about her earlier public speech I asked her where she bought her shirts from as she wears cowboy-style shirts, invariably with horses embroidered on them. As my daughter is an avid horse rider I thought I might purchase one on the Internet. The conversation was brief but indicates Temple's difficulties:

Kate Wall: *You always wear the most beautiful shirts and I would like to buy one for my daughter. Where do you buy them from?*

Temple Grandin: *The shirt shop.*

While her response clearly answered the question posed it did not help me as I needed the name of the shop. She also gave me a rather bemused look as if I was asking a rather ridiculous question, which in her eyes of course I was. I then continued to ask her the name of the shirt shop and she responded appropriately. Her initial response indicates her lack of ability to deduce what specific information I was seeking. Another area of difficulty Temple talks about is her inability to know when to enter a conversation as she understands the basic rules of communication, such as you should wait until someone finishes before you respond, but is never quite sure when the time is right. Invariably this ends up with her not joining in conversations she actually wants to participate in. So we can begin to understand that while an individual with an ASD may be a fluent speaker it does not necessarily follow that they are an effective communicator. This is significant in our own work with adolescents and adults with ASDs.

For some individuals with ASDs the fact they can understand everything that is said to them but are unable to speak produces additional difficulties. Although this tends to happen during childhood it can, for some, remain through adulthood. The resulting frustration can often manifest as unacceptable behaviour such as screaming, head banging, self-harming or violence to others.

For the individuals we work with or care for in adolescence and adulthood there is likely to have been a lack of speech and language therapy during their childhood combined with a lack of awareness and understanding of ASDs, so appropriate and early help may have been denied them. Our task is to try to enable communication, at whatever level is appropriate for the individual, which will enable them to become more independent. Another communication difficulty for some individuals with ASDs who have developed limited verbal skills is echolalia, when they repeat what was said to them as a response. This, however, may be interpreted as them understanding what was said but in reality it is more likely that they do not understand what is being asked of them or are stressed by the situation but know that a response will be expected so simply repeat the latter part of the question to the speaker. This, they hope, will satisfy the speaker, who will then move away and an uncertain and uncomfortable situation will have been avoided. As a simple example:

Speaker: *Do you want a cup of tea?*

Adult with ASD: *... cup of tea.*

Speaker: *Okay, I'll make you one.*

The adult may not have understood the question or want a drink at all or wants an alternative drink but simply cannot cope with the 'confrontational' nature of a conversation. However, the speaker has assumed understanding. When speaking, individuals with ASDs may use a stilted, monotonous or unusual tone which some people may find difficult to understand. We all use varied pitch, tone and intonation to emphasise aspects of our speech but this may not be so for those with ASDs.

When confronted with someone who wants to engage in conversation some people with ASDs will react negatively. This is because the speaker will usually be looking at their eyes and they know that they will be expected to respond. The eye contact may make them feel very uncomfortable and the expectation to respond may prove too much. This could result in hand flapping, placing hands over ears or banging the ears (blocking out the sound), placing hands over eyes (to avoid eye contact), walking away, rocking and so on. If this is the case for an individual then why do we persist in trying to engage them in conversation? If we were constantly confronted with a situation we feel uncomfortable with surely we would probably also avoid such situations in the future.

Understanding gestures, body language and facial expressions are also areas of difficulty. We all use gestures, body language and facial expressions during conversation. We also interpret other people's body language when we see them, so we can assess if they are relaxed and comfortable in a situation or not.

For individuals with ASDs this is not something that comes easily and for some will never develop. We therefore need to think carefully about the way we use our faces and bodies during conversation as this can confuse the individual and possibly make them more stressed. Another aspect of our own conversation is the common use of familiar sayings and idioms which can confuse individuals with ASDs as their understanding is more literal. Typical examples would include:

- *get your skates on* – meaning *hurry up*. The individual with an ASD may think 'I haven't got any skates so what does she want me to do?'

- *Pull your socks up* – meaning *try harder*.

- *Jump in the bath* – meaning *get in the bath*, not get in the bath and jump up and down.

- *Let's have a butcher's* – meaning *let's have a look/show me*.

We should therefore be careful of the terminology we use to avoid unnecessary confusion.

For individuals who have developed fluent speech, understanding of communication and conversation may be more difficult for them to grasp. If they have a particular stereotypical interest (often bordering on the obsessional) they may greet you and immediately start talking about their favourite subject. This one-sided 'lecture' could go on for a considerable time and they may show no signs of bringing it to an end. This way they are in control of the situation and are avoiding being asked anything they do not understand or which may confuse them, but clearly this is not effective and purposeful conversation, let alone a two-way interaction. However, to stop them mid-flow may cause them distress, so handling such situations is a delicate issue. If we also reflect on the possibilities of hearing issues, some individuals may also be more confused in conversation as they find it difficult to block out the other noises and sounds they can hear and therefore cannot concentrate on the speaker's voice. In a secondary classroom situation an adolescent with such hearing difficulties may hear everything that is happening in the corridor outside and outside the window, so be unable to focus on what the teacher is saying. Studying is therefore much harder for such students. Gillingham (1995: 51) cites a useful example to clarify understanding:

> Why do you think I have so much trouble paying attention in the classroom? I hear everything that goes on – every phone call that the principal makes in her office; every single time an eighteen-wheeler truck gears down on the highway three blocks away. I HEAR IT! I HEAR EVERYTHING! I hear people talking outside the school building, and I can understand their conversations. There are so many noises in my head that I can't concentrate on what Mrs Weaver tries to say. I can't focus and pay attention to the teacher's spoken words – I'm too distracted. AND, why do you think I'm so tired all the time? It takes so much energy to pay attention that I am worn out. I TRY SO HARD AND I JUST CAN'T DO IT!!! (Nicholas Bober)

Imagination

Imagination beyond the here and now may be limited in adolescents and adults with autism. They are unlikely to have developed imaginative play in childhood, preferring to restrict their play to familiar routines and structure. For example, as a child a young boy may have been obsessed with Thomas the Tank Engine but restricted his play to driving it back and forth in a straight line, which could engage him for hours if not distracted to an alternative activity. He would not have engaged in building a train track and laying it out differently each time he played with it nor would he have developed stories to act out with the train. Any play outside of the child's accepted routine would not have emerged and he could be very resistant if changes were introduced by others (children or adults).

Similarly, with an adolescent at secondary school the uncertainties of a science laboratory and experimentation may produce considerable stress, yet be a part of the curriculum to be followed by all students. Within the residential care home you may have followed a chocolate cake recipe with a resident several times with great success, but if you suggest changing the ingredients on the recipe to make a coffee cake you may be asking too much. However, if you typed up a recipe for a coffee cake and presented it as something new to try it is more likely to be accepted. It is simply knowledge and understanding that can change the way we approach activities that can make the world of difference to the individual with an ASD, for whom most of their daily life can be fraught with uncertainty, anxiety, frustration and stress.

This need for sameness and routine is typical of most individuals with ASDs so any changes in daily life must be prepared for or the resulting stress and anxiety can manifest as difficult or unacceptable behaviour. It may be that the individual always has to be first into the classroom or dining room or always has to have the same plates, cups, mugs, glasses and cutlery. Yet if this is the case, why not allow them to have this? Why create additional problems for an individual who finds daily life confusing enough. I have worked with families who have arrangements with local eating places whereby they ring up and book 'their' table and have left at the restaurant their own identical set of crockery and cutlery. Knowing the table will be laid virtually the same as at home can offer the individual the security of familiarity that enables the family to engage in an activity that most families would take for granted.

Daily routine is a necessity for most individuals with ASDs and with the help of structure, routine, lists and timetables many difficulties can be overcome. As we will see in Chapter 6, the TEACCH (Treatment and Education of Autistic and Related Communication Handicapped Children) and SPELL (National Autistic Society) approaches advocate visual supporting techniques for all individuals with ASDs and this can provide the backdrop for a calmer daily life. If the individual is generally calmer and confident within their routine then it is more likely that progress can be made in many areas. A basic activity such as the early morning routine for an adult with an ASD may cause significant distress but by implementing a timetable (see case studies below) and teaching them to follow it, unnecessary stress and frustration can be eliminated. The amount of detail on the timetable can be adapted according to the needs of the individual.

Case study 4.3 Morning routine timetable

1   Get out of bed and go to bathroom.

2   Go to toilet.

3   Run warm water in the sink.

4   Take off pyjama top.

5   Wet your flannel and rub soap onto it.

6   Wash your face, neck, chest, arms and hands.

7   Use the towel to dry yourself.

8   Wet your toothbrush and put some toothpaste on it.

9   Clean all your teeth thoroughly.

10 Rinse your mouth with clean water and spit it into the sink.

11 Go back to your room.

12 Get undressed and put clean clothes on:

    (a) pants

    (b) socks

    (c) shirt

    (d) trousers

    (e) jumper.

13 Brush your hair.

14 Go downstairs to eat breakfast.

Case study 4.4 Morning routine timetable

- Go to bathroom.
- Use toilet, wash, clean your teeth and brush your hair.
- Go back to your room and get dressed.
- Go downstairs for breakfast.

Another area of resistance to change can be seen with some individuals' refusal to try new foods or eat certain foods or textures of food. In more extreme cases this may result in the elimination of so many types of food that the remaining diet lacks nourishment and goodness. The possible oversensitivity to taste may also impact on food issues and individuals may be physically sick if made to eat certain foods or combinations of food they do not feel they can tolerate. An example would be an adult who liked ham and tomato sauce sandwiches, but had to have it presented as one piece of bread and butter with tomato sauce on, placed next to another piece of bread and butter placed next to a slice of ham. He was not able to put them together and eat them as a whole sandwich. Others may dissect food on the plate to ascertain what exactly it is comprised of before eating it. Of course when in public or eating with new people this can appear to be unorthodox, but if fellow diners are forewarned this can be overcome, or we could check a menu beforehand and ensure there will be options available that are unlikely to cause difficulties.

Linked to poor imaginative skills as well as social interaction skills are the inability of individuals with ASDs to understand and appreciate other people's feelings and emotions. Within their own lives other people are largely unnecessary, need little consideration and therefore they have no need to understand and respect their feelings. This, however, can result in them being considered inconsiderate, selfish, rude or disrespectful.

Other behaviours associated with autism

Individuals with ASDs may demonstrate one or more of the following behaviours:

- unusual body movements such as walking on tiptoes, flapping hands, detailed and repetitive finger movements, rocking and swaying
- head banging, self-biting or other self-injurious behaviours–to the point of causing significant injury
- unusual special interests bordering on obsessions.

Those developing a special interest such as train timetables, mathematical calculations, calendar dates or even a familiar television programme may develop their knowledge to a level beyond normal expectation and in a few instances can excel beyond our understanding. These skills can develop to such a high level of perfection that they would be beyond the capabilities of other experts in the field. Such individuals are known as *autistic savants*. An example is Stephen Wiltshire who, as an adult with an ASD, has severe learning difficulties in other areas and very limited speech yet can reproduce pencil drawings and paintings with extraordinary brilliance. To see his work is to observe superb artistic quality and when one considers that he can view a building such as Buckingham Palace for a few minutes then go away and produce an accurate reproduction on paper is quite amazing. The accuracy is astounding even down to the exact number of windows. Stephen occasionally exhibits in London and the exhibition is well worthy of a visit for anyone with an interest in this particular aspect of ASDs. His work has also been reproduced in a book (Wiltshire, 1991), in which the inside cover informs us that:

What makes these drawings truly extraordinary is the fact that Wiltshire is autistic – as in the character played by Dustin Hoffman in *Rain Man* – and lives within his own private world. Yet his remarkable drawings express an understanding of his surroundings that most of us would envy. Not only does his art reveal expert craftsmanship and a mastery of perspective, but more important, it reveals his mysterious creative ability to capture the feeling of a building, its mood, character and voice.

Sensory difficulties

Sensory difficulties can affect the individual in the areas of touch, vision, hearing, taste and/or smell. Evidence to date is now building into a viable explanation for many of the unusual behaviours that we link with autism. Gillingham's work (1995) explores this area in depth and offers the following insight:

> According to some individuals with autism, their disability is linked directly to the senses. They describe how the touch of another human being can be so excruciating, smells can be overpowering, hearing can hurt, sight that is distorted, and tastes that may be too strong. The world of the person with autism can be a world of pain. The development of the autistic personality is their method of coping with the pain. (p.12)

Gillingham's *sensory theory of autism* suggests that individuals with autism find ways to cope with the pain they feel and that the behaviours we observe as odd or unusual are in fact to reduce the pain levels. She contends that those with ASDs can produce extra endorphins (biochemicals produced in the brain) through repeating certain behaviours such as hand flapping, rocking and so on. The extra endorphins created set up a barrier against the pain and effectively block it out. If required they can develop the ability to totally overload their senses and thus 'shut down' their senses when faced with extremely difficult sensory situations. Reflecting on some of the examples offered previously in this book we can see that the sensory theory makes much sense and thus we need to consider this area in our work with individuals with ASDs.

Summary

Throughout this chapter the key areas of difficulty experienced by those with ASDs have been highlighted with examples offered to deepen understanding. With this knowledge of the characteristics of an ASD and increased awareness of the world of autism it is hoped that we will be better placed to create improved individual planning systems to enable success for all adolescents and adults we work with. If society is unable to understand and accept individuals with ASDs then we as their education, health and care providers have a responsibility to provide appropriately using our own understanding to enable appropriate activities for each and every person we meet.

Key issues

❖ Parents and practitioners need to have considerable knowledge of the effects of ASDs on those they support in order to provide effectively.

❖ This raises issues of training, access to training and therefore funding, as all professionals and carers should have access to such training and information.

❖ With appropriate knowledge professionals can respond to the individual needs of adolescents and adults with ASDs.

Suggestions for discussion (professionals)

1. Consider an individual you are currently working with or have worked with in the past and list the key behaviours they demonstrate in the areas of: social interaction, social communication, imagination. Identify any changes you may wish to make to your provision in the light of new knowledge gained from reading this chapter.

2. Does everyone working with you have a thorough understanding of the characteristics of ASDs? If not, what can be done to address this?

Suggestions for discussion (parents)

1. List the key behaviours your son/daughter demonstrates in the areas of: social interaction, social communication, imagination. Identify any changes you might wish to make to the way you behave with them in the light of new knowledge gained from this chapter.

2. Think about how you can ensure that the professionals working with your son/daughter are knowledgeable of these issues and are providing appropriately, as consistency between home and their workplace will be essential.

 ## Suggested further reading

Gillingham, G. (1995) *Autism. Handle with Care!* Arlington, TX: Future Horizons.

Peeters, T. (1997) *Autism: From Theoretical Understanding to Educational Intervention.* London: Whurr.

Website–Temple Grandin: www.autism.org/temple/inside

5

Considering family issues

This chapter explores:
- ➤ the effects of ASDs on family members;
- ➤ issues from the childhood of the member with an ASD which have a long-term impact on the family;
- ➤ issues for professional to consider;
- ➤ key areas of concern for family members relating to the adult with ASD.

Introduction

We are, quite rightly, likely to spend considerable time discussing and debating current policy and practice in our attempts to ensure effective provision for all young people and adults with ASDs we work with. Yet each individual student, resident or client will have been, or will still be, central to his/her own family. Throughout their childhood the majority of children with ASDs are resident with their families and the difficulties and issues related to ASDs as they grow into adults, as explored in Chapter 4, are likely to have had a significant impact on the family. Research evidence supports this view (e.g. Loynes, 2001a; Internet 1):

> A child with autism will have a significant impact on the lives of family members and it is important to consider all the options as objectively as possible. There is, however, no one answer and each family needs to be considered as an individual unit. (Internet 1)

In addition the parental role in decision-making processes has steadily increased over the past 20 years, so professionals have a responsibility to reflect on parental perspectives as well as their views and feelings about the services and provision we offer.

We should always remember that we, as professionals, have chosen our career path and have selected to work with young people or adults with ASDs. In addition we work an average 40-hour week and then return to our own families. For parents there has invariably been no such choice. The current situation with their son/daughter with an ASD was not expected and will be with them 24 hours every day. I do acknowledge that that there are some professionals who have a son or daughter with learning disabilities but clearly for the majority this is not the case.

Diagnosis and childhood: experiences of the family

When expecting a baby, parents and other family members will begin a process of changing emotions, feelings and considerations for the future including discussions around names for the child, curiosity regarding the sex of the child, the health of the mother and baby during pregnancy and the birth itself, schools, financial changes, employment changes, family life changes and so on. Many plans for the future will be debated and decided upon. The impact of a diagnosis for any child's condition or disorder is likely to create a variety of feelings and emotions in any parent. If the diagnosis occurs at or before birth the feelings of the parents may suddenly be changed. Their ideas for their future lives may now look very different and the child they were expecting is now to be an 'unexpected' child – the unexpected child that may not achieve the same outcomes, may not attend the local nursery and mainstream schools and may need constant care into adulthood. Emily Pearl's description (see below) of this period of unexpected change clarifies beautifully the significance of changes that occur but also the need to accept the changed pathway which may be different, but may not be as difficult as first thought and will offer its own rewards and delights.

Case Study 5.1 Welcome to Holland by Emily Pearl

I am often asked to describe the experience of having a disability or a huge disappointment in life – to try to help people who have not had this experience to understand it, to imagine how it feels.

When you're planning your life and your retirement, it's like planning a fabulous vacation trip to Italy. You save your money, buy a bunch of guidebooks and make your wonderful plans – the Coliseum, the Michelangelo, David and the gondolas in Venice. You may learn some handy phrases in Italian. It's all very exciting.

After months of eager anticipation, the day finally arrives. Your bags are packed and off you go. Several hours later, the plane lands. The stewardess comes in and says, 'Welcome to Holland.'

'Holland?!' you say. 'What do you mean, Holland? I signed up for Italy! I'm supposed to be in Italy. All my life I've dreamed and planned for a trip to Italy!'

But there's been a change in the flight plan. They've landed in Holland and there you must stay. The important thing is that they haven't taken you to a horrible, filthy place full of pestilence, famine and disease. It's just a different place. It's slower paced than Italy, less flashy than Italy.

But after you've been there a while, and you catch your breath, you look around and you begin to notice that Holland has windmills. Holland has tulips. Holland has Rembrandts. So you must go out and buy new guidebooks. And you must learn a whole new language. And you will meet a whole new group of people you would never have met.

But everyone you know is busy coming and going from Italy, and they're all bragging about what a wonderful time they had there. And for the rest of your life, you will say, 'Yes, that's where I was supposed to go. That's what I had planned.' And the pain of that will never, ever, ever go away, because the loss of that dream is a very significant loss.

But if you spend your life mourning that you didn't get to Italy, you may never be free to enjoy the very special, the very lovely things about Holland.

(Internet 15)

The range of feelings experienced by parents at the time of diagnosis (whether at birth or later) could include loss, grief, denial, acceptance, anxiety, confusion and/or guilt. We should also remember that the mother and father may not work through their own emotions at the same time or even experience the same emotions at the same time. This can lead to considerable frustration, anxiety and stress and at this time both parents will need appropriate support.

Specific issues for fathers

A concern specifically identified by fathers is 'marginalisation', as highlighted by Carpenter (1997) who concluded that fathers of children with disabilities felt an expectation to be the parent who would, as society expects, support the mother. At no time were the father's own needs of support acknowledged or addressed. Many also admitted to returning to work earlier than planned to reintroduce some normality into their lives. Yet professional meetings and appointments with parents are mainly held during professional working hours, thus automatically excluding many fathers. These arrangements may suit us, the professionals, but we are then responsible for excluding fathers from participation in these essential discussions. Beyond the range of issues relating to fathers we should also reflect on the effects on grandparents, siblings and extended family.

Parents

For a parent of a child with an ASD the same range of emotions and feelings will have been experienced but these will often be compounded if the child appeared to have been developing according to expected developmental patterns initially and then experienced a period of, often rapid, regression. Throughout the regressive period the parents may be confused with what is happening and unable to make sense of it. If it is their first child then they may consider this a period of stagnant development which will pick up again given time and the reality becomes very difficult to accept and to comprehend. Such difficulties are often further compounded by the confusion arising from the likelihood of having to fit in and see an array of specialists before a diagnosis is secured.

While diagnoses of autism have increased substantially over the years there are still some professionals who appear reluctant to label the condition or mis-diagnose, leading to additional complications. Bill Davis, the father of a boy with an ASD, described his own experiences at this time: 'So we set out on our burdensome journey of psychiatrist, neurologists, MRIs and hearing tests. We scheduled things very quickly, but it still took a few months to follow through with all the appointments' (2001: 35). He goes on to describe the ongoing battles that followed when trying to secure appropriate educational provision – another potential battlefield for parents.

Charlotte Moore, herself the mother of three children, two of whom have autism, summarises her experiences:

> Dr S was a cold fish. I knew what he was going to say before he said it, so I was able to sit and listen to him and think, in a detached way, you're not making a bad job of this, Dr S. 'Yes, he's on the autistic spectrum all right,' he said. I was sitting with my chair against the door to prevent Sam escaping. Sam was behind the doctor. He had licked a fruit pastille and was tracing patterns with it, like sticky snail trails, all over the back of the doctor's chair. The pastille was inching ever closer to Dr S's tweed jacket. 'But I wouldn't worry too much,' continued Dr S. 'They can be very intelligent, you know. Some of them go to Eton.' I smiled and nodded, but I thought perhaps I wouldn't put Sam's name down for Eton quite yet. (2004: 88)

The NAS report *Opening the Door* (1999) reported the findings of a survey of National Autistic Society members and highlighted a range of problems experienced surrounding diagnosis:

- 40 per cent of parents had to wait over three years to get a diagnosis (p. 9).

- 65 per cent of parents saw three or more professionals before securing a diagnosis, with 23 per cent seeing five or more (p. 13).

- 45 per cent of parents stated that the disability was described inadequately or not at all. In addition, 81 per cent stated that there was either no assessment of severity at all or a vague assessment (p. 17).

- 43 per cent were dissatisfied to some degree with the diagnostic process with 22 per cent being very dissatisfied (p. 18).

- 43 per cent reported they were not given any advice about where to go for help/support/counselling or further explanation (p. 19).

- 49 per cent reported that the support they received at the time of diagnosis was inadequate (p. 19).

For the typical family the impact of the child with an ASD will be far reaching and powerful. The difficulties experienced by children with an ASD often manifest as unusual, unacceptable and sometimes bizarre behaviours and this can result in significant problems when participating in everyday family life outside of the home. As a result families have reported that they become increasingly isolated as invitations to barbecues, birthday parties and get-togethers with similar families tend to decline. In addition the reactions of the general public to a child that shows no outward signs of having an ASD can be very negative and damaging. Ordinary family experiences such as going to the pictures or the park, holidays, going to cafes or restaurants, shopping in town can each be periods of extreme difficulty and stress for each and every family member.

The resulting behaviours and stress and anxiety they cause can often be more than some parents are prepared to cope with and they end up having shopping delivered and/or the child remaining at home. In this way families, and especially siblings, can be significantly affected by the child with an ASD.

Siblings

Siblings have also reported a range of significant issues that having a brother or sister with an ASD has placed on their own lives:

- reluctance often to bring friends home
- resentful of the attention the sibling receives and the lack of parental attention they receive
- the inability to share everyday family experiences outside of the house
- embarrassment when in public
- lack of support and information available for siblings
- interference by the child with autism in the activities of the sibling within the home – taking things, tearing or breaking possessions, spoiling games and play, physical aggression (often more severe than normal sibling aggression)
- feeling the need to 'escape' into their own space, e.g. locking themselves in their bedrooms, which can lead to increased isolation
- pressures to succeed as their sibling is less likely to achieve high levels of success
- a need for everyday activities without the sibling's presence to achieve a sense of 'normal' family life
- alternatively, feelings of great love and an increased sensitivity to the needs of those with disabilities.

Over the past 15 to 20 years the expansion of the World Wide Web has seen the growth of accessible information and support for siblings of children with ASDs, including websites provided by charitable and government organisations as well as independent sites run by individuals. There are now many independent sites, created by and written by and for siblings of people with ASDs which offer contact with others in similar situations and with similar experiences. Such sites allow a sibling to explore and discuss their own feelings and difficulties within a supportive and non-judgemental environment, and with people who are likely to understand exactly how they feel. This does, however, assume that every sibling has access to the Internet. Yet how much support has been offered by the government and local services to address the needs of all siblings across the whole of the UK?

Parental employment issues

In many families, one parent (often the mother) is placed in a situation where plans to return to her chosen career have to be reconsidered as the child needs looking after every day and childcare facilities that can accommodate his/her needs can be very difficult to find, if at all. This situation may well continue into adulthood. In such situations the mother is likely to feel that she has little choice but to remain at home, which may cause resentment and psychological difficulties. Parents who have reported such difficulties (see Internet 1; Loynes, 2001a) feel that the lack of support and alternatives available for parents forces them into a situation that results in considerable financial loss for the family as well as adding pressure, anxiety and stress. Loynes (2001a) discovered:

> A survey of carers with a paid job and carers without found that, of those who worked, nearly three quarters said that their earnings were affected by caring. Their average annual loss was £5,625. Carers without a paid job had an average annual loss of £9,763. (p. 12)

As well as this loss of income, through no fault of their own, the welfare benefit system does not currently make up the shortfall in the income to the household so the family of a child with an ASD is heavily penalised. Specialist care for their child, if available, is also likely to be costly so a double penalty emerges.

Educational issues

Moving onto the educational phase, Loynes' report (2001b) highlighted similar family issues linked to educational provision for children and adolescents with ASDs:

- 87% of respondents perceive an increase in the number of children diagnosed with ASD over the last five years.
- Only 25% of children with ASD have statement.
- Over 10% of all children with a Statement of Educational Needs have ASD.

- Many LEA's appear unable to measure either training levels or needs, and so there is no coherent authority-wide strategy for pupils with ASD. (p. 1)

Many parents expressed dissatisfaction with the range of provision and appropriateness to meet the individual needs of their own child with an ASD. A NAS survey of schools (2002: 7) concluded that:

- 44% of schools which identified children with autistic spectrum disorders say that significant numbers of them are not getting the specialist support they need.
- 55% of those responding felt that support was not forthcoming because of problems or delays with diagnosis or statementing. Around a third (30%) of respondents mentioned insufficient resources, both human and financial.
- 47% of those responding would like to see training and advice provided by or through the LEA.
- 31% of schools with pupils with autistic spectrum disorders have no speech and language therapy.

In addition they reported that: '72% of schools were dissatisfied with the extent of their teacher's training in autism' (ibid.: 7).

If we reflect on the issues these facts raise and their impact on the families we can begin to understand the 'battles' they may have fought throughout their child's education, from primary school through to secondary school and beyond. The impact for the family is likely to have included:

- difficulties securing a diagnosis
- no immediate offers of appropriate support and/or placement following diagnosis
- continuous dealings with the school(s) and/or the local authority to secure an appropriate school placement
- continuous discussions about securing qualified, knowledgeable and appropriate teaching input
- significant difficulties attempting to secure speech and language therapy.

Each of the above will have placed additional burdens on the parents and would have likely led to further anxiety and stress way beyond the usual stresses and strains of bringing up children.

While the government may have in place a process of increasing inclusion in mainstream schools the realities of providing appropriate educational opportunities for children with ASDs is a world apart. The government would argue that they have the SEN Code of Practice and Guidance for Autistic Spectrum Disorders to support staff, yet the gulf between policy and practice is considerable. Challenges and barriers exist for schools and considerably more thought and support needs to be implemented, through national training, to improve the current situation.

The situation for those in secondary schools does not improve and some parents would argue that it gets worse the older the child gets. The teenager with an ASD will find the practicalities of a timetable in a secondary school very difficult to cope with and the need to have the right equipment on the right day will be a further challenge for many. For those who usually rely on 'sameness' and consistency in their lives to suddenly be faced with different rooms and teachers for every lesson will be very stressful and pose a range of problems. Securing ASD-appropriate help will also be somewhat of a postcode lottery and may predominantly depend on the teenager meeting one or two teachers along the way who do have a wealth of knowledge and experience in ASDs and know exactly how to support them. So for parents the battles are ongoing as they support their child through the transition to secondary education, fight to secure appropriate support and deal with potential bullying as their child is perceived as different, all of which are typical problems identified by families and which again place continued pressures on the family unit that has already had the battles of diagnosis and primary education to cope with.

An additional complication lies in the increases in early diagnosis meaning that more and more children with ASDs are now proceeding through the education system and into adulthood – but can the secondary schools and the support services for adults cope with this expected demand? The NAS report *Autism in Schools: Crisis or Challenge?* (Barnard et al., 2002: 25) concluded that:

> Regardless of whether the underlying rate is increasing, there are more children with autistic spectrum disorders in English and Welsh schools than ever previously reported. Resources must be found to meet the needs of these children if the policy of inclusion is to work in practice. The government must act now to fund training and employ qualified and specialist practitioners to prevent the failure of the policy of educational inclusion. Continuing to place children with autistic spectrum disorders in mainstream classrooms without adequate support places unfair pressure on teachers. For the child in question, it will lead to integration without social inclusion or educational progress at best, and destructive behaviour and exclusion from school in the worst cases.

This damning indictment of current government policy indicates the results of poorly planned and delivered educational changes that place unrelentless pressures on the children themselves, the teachers and the parents of the children. At a time of additional pressure from league tables the situation is further exacerbated for all concerned. The additional pressures indirectly placed on the parents of the children are unacceptable and are likely to cause ongoing and prolonged misery, possibly leading to long-term depression and anxiety. Thankfully many parents of children and young people with ASDs become their child's campaigner and will stop at nothing in their attempts to secure appropriate support and provision for their child. But should we not be ensuring that all the needs of the children and their families are met by current policies and practice in a proactive manner rather than trying to deal with the outcomes of a service that does not meet the needs of all children and young people with ASDs?

Issues of further and higher education

For those who are able, we now have more and more young people with ASDs securing places for continued studies. These may be vocational or basic skills courses or higher-level academic courses and qualifications. By the time the young person has reached 14+ they should have access to the Connexions service in which personal advisers work with young people aged 14–19 offering information, advice and support relating to any issues that may be affecting them at home, school, college or work. For young people with special needs the Connexions advisers can continue support till age 25. Typically, in Year 9 of secondary school (age 14) students will make choices about their school subject choices for the next two years (GCSE years) and the local Connexions partnership will be able to advise and support students. Similarly at age 16, another range of options emerges – staying on at school, transferring to college or leaving school and entering the workplace. For the young person with an ASD each of these stages of transition will need to be supported by people in schools and the Connexions services who have a good understanding of ASDs or the advice and support may not be appropriate. Parents again may need to 'supervise' each stage carefully and offer advice to the schools and Connexions advisers regarding the very specific needs of their child. Current changes in educational and more specifically curriculum policy for 14–19 year olds should mean that by 2009 there will be wider and possibly more appropriate options for those students who have not achieved academically to follow more vocational programmes to ensure they have the basic skills to enter the workforce. However, for some young people with ASDs this may not be possible or appropriate without considerable training of the staff responsible.

Issues relating to HE are similar to FE – success will largely depend on the awareness of individual academic tutors as well as the Disability Officer who should work with the parents and the student from the start. Additional support packages are available to all students with disabilities including study support tutors, student mentors, computer packages and so on. Yet again, knowledge of the needs of these individuals with ASDs will play a central role in the pathway to success and parents may need to offer more support from 'afar' through regular contact with either the support staff, personal tutor and/or their son/daughter. The social difficulties allied to ASDs often result in the student not engaging in the social life of the university to the full extent – they may be much happier staying in their room on campus or studying in the library or computer suites as this avoids having to engage too much with their peers. In this respect students with ASDs, while securing their degrees or diplomas, may be missing out on what is often considered a very significant aspect of university life. HE studying also invariably involves moving away from home and leading a more independent life, although the academic tutoring fees now charged tends to result in more students studying nearer to home to ease the financial burden.

While the adult may well be living away from home in a reasonably independent manner parents are still likely to worry about their son/daughter as they will be quite vulnerable in this new, exciting but often confusing environment and they will not be overseeing their lives as before. The 'not knowing' is often more worrying for any parent than the reality of what is happening, particularly where their child (albeit grown up) is concerned.

Recent figures relating to exclusions from education indicate that those with ASDs are excluded at a rate that is twenty times higher than the national average (Barnard et al., 2001), and this is invariably due to their unpredictable or extreme behaviour patterns. However, the behaviours that result in exclusions may in fact be the outcome of the school or college's inability to respond effectively to the needs of all pupils with ASD's not the young person's inability to conform to accepted behaviour patterns as can be seen in the case study below.

Case study 5.2 Joanne

Joanne is 15 and has particular difficulties with hypersensitivity and cannot concentrate or remain on task when in an inappropriate situation with excessive sensory stimulation. Her mathematics class is situated in the classroom next to the gym and she can hear the water of the showers, the students' conversations in the showers, the teacher's raised voice, the raised screams of some of the students in the changing rooms, as well as all the conversations being held by people walking past the outside of her classroom. She finds it very difficult to concentrate on what the teacher is saying despite her best efforts.

Some students at the back of the class are passing a note forwards so the student behind Joanne taps her on the back to pass the note along, which startles her. The cumulative effect of trying to cope with all the noises and sounds she can hear, plus the distraction from the person seated behind her, as well as trying to concentrate becomes overpowering. Joanne turns around and pushes the student behind her out of his chair, hits him and pushes his desk over before storming out of the room. The teacher summons the head teacher who informs Joanne that as this is the umpteenth time she has behaved this way he has no choice but to give her a temporary exclusion as she is a danger to her fellow pupils.

Key issues:

1 Identify the factors leading up to Joanne's exclusion?

2 Who was to blame for the situation?

3 Reflect on the issues this will raise for Joanne's family.

So again, for parents and families of young people with ASDs, there may be continued and ongoing transitions to support which create additional problems and stresses for the young person and which thus affect the family members as well.

Adulthood

As we have seen the reality for many young people with ASDs is that they do not generally do well at school, college or university, despite any help (appropriate or otherwise) that may have been offered, and for many, despite everything their parents have fought for. So what happens in adulthood and how does this affect the family?

Employment

For most individuals with a disability the issue of finding and maintaining paid employment is a significant one and for those with ASDs this is no different. Employers would need to be understanding of and aware of ASD issues, the impact on the individual and others working in the same environment and the need to support the individual in perhaps a different way than is usual. Having said that, many adults with an ASD, as long as they have a supportive employer, can be exceptionally loyal and hard-working employees. The key difficulties associated with an ASD are social interaction, social communication and imagination, so the individual with an ASD is likely to be very happy with the same route to work every day, the same desk which is laid out in his/her way and the routine tasks of a job. Each of these offers the sameness and consistency preferred and means they are likely to remain on task and be less likely to want to engage in much conversation in the photocopying room or across desks. Those large office environments with separated desk areas resemble the work stations advocated in the TEACCH approach so are well suited to support those adults with an ASD that are able to hold down a job in staying on task and performing the set agenda of tasks. To this end jobs that do not require a great deal of verbal communication and have a set pattern of tasks to be completed are highly suitable. Similarly, computer-based jobs are often suitable as the employee does not need to engage with others due to the one-to-one interaction with the computer occupying most of their day. If an employer or manager can provide the employee with a list of tasks that need to be completed then the employee is likely to settle down and work through the list quite happily. Alternative employment opportunities could include working in libraries, working in kitchens, factory work, accountancy (due to mathematical preferences), general administrative tasks and so on – anywhere where there exists a routine to the job and limited communication skills are needed would be suitable. So employment opportunities do exist, and for school-leavers or younger adults with ASDs the careers office, jobcentre or Connexions service should be able to support the transition into the workplace by way of a supportive, mentoring role throughout the start of the new job till the employee feels confident of their responsibilities and the requirements that will be placed on them.

So if employment opportunities do exist, how is it that Barnard et al. (2001: 7) highlighted that 'only 12% of higher functioning adults are in full-time paid employment and 24% are doing nothing or are helping out around the house', and Howlin (2004: 233) concluded that:

> The majority of placements that were found were menial and poorly paid, in positions such as kitchen hands, unskilled factory workers, or backroom super-market staff. In addition, jobs had often been procured through the efforts or personal contacts of family members rather than through the proper channels.

Yet those individuals with ASDs that want to secure employment readily voice their views:

> 'I want a "proper" job. Full-time employment.'

> 'Preferably not doing unpaid voluntary work and instead working in a full-time permanent position in my chosen field.'

> > Adults cited in Barnard et al.'s report (2001: 18)

Clearly the system is not working appropriately to support the needs of all adults with ASDs that are capable of securing employment, so this should be addressed. The potential outcomes would be that of increased independence, reductions in welfare benefits received, enhanced self-esteem, personal satisfaction and relieving the pressure and stress on the family. To experience the battles of trying to secure appropriate education for your child as they grow up and then to find there are limited job opportunities must be devastating for parents and cannot be beneficial to their own ongoing health and well-being.

The government strategy Valuing People (DoH, 2001b) '... believes that employment is an important route to social inclusion and that all those who wish to work should have the opportunities and support to do so' (p. 84). So clearly the government appears committed to supporting and encouraging those with ASDs to secure employment but there exist discrete differences in suggesting strategies to support those with learning disabilities and those with ASDs. However, the New Workstep Programme 'will benefit people with learning disabilities' (DoH, 2001b: 85) and 'Learning Disability Partnership Boards will develop local employment strategies' (ibid.). With these in place time will tell to see if the current 'less than 10% of people with learning disabilities are in employment' (DoH, 2002: 84) will increase. It will then be interesting to see that, if there is an increase, how many of these will be adults with ASDs.

Employment will be revisited in Chapter 8.

Housing

Barnard et al.'s report (2001: 18) shows that nearly 50 per cent of adults with ASDs still live at home with just over 30 per cent living in residential settings. Only 3–4 per cent lived independently and another 85 per cent lived semi-independently. Thus the impact on the family extends well into adulthood and for many becomes permanent. The more recent report by Harker and King (2004) reminds us of the increase in diagnosis of children with ASDs, which will result in a dire shortage of appropriate provision when they become adults. Their stark message (2004: 6) is: 'The numbers of children being diagnosed with an autistic spectrum disorder suggest that the scale of need for adult services must be established quickly if they are not to be overtaken by a crisis in demand.'

Conversely it could be suggested that some parents have a perceived need to continue caring for their adult child and have adapted well to their roles as primary care-givers. They may not consider that any other providers could offer such high-quality and individually tailored provision for their son/daughter and do not therefore wish for or encourage their son/daughter to embark on an independent life. Grant (2005 et al.: 234) suggest:

> ... it is still not clear whether such parents are effectively captive and dependent, for economic, physical and psychological reasons, upon keeping their disabled adult child at home.

For those adults with ASDs capable of moving away from home there will need to be a carefully planned transition stage involving possibly many visits to the new accommodation before embarking on the move itself. Harker and King (2004) identified the criticality of this transition period and highlighted the following challenges relating to accommodation for adults with ASDs:

> The challenge for the next 5 years is:
> - A better understanding of the range of existing need and provision
> - An improvement in the choice available
> - Information and help for people and their families seeking to plan for the future
> - Strategies for services in the light of Valuing People to include autism
> - To use the Supporting People programme for a wide range of housing needs. (p. 6)

The White Paper *Valuing People* (DoH, 2001b) is key in raising the profile of this important issue for adults with ASDs, stating that the government aim is 'to enable people with learning disabilities and their families to have greater choice and control over where and how they live' (p. 70). One of the key aspects for the future outlined in the report was the commitment of the government to make available £10 billion for housing capital costs for three years after the report was published. As a result of recent trends and government initiatives there are now more adults with learning disabilities moving out of their family home into accommodation – either into a care home, supported living or independently – but much more still needs to be done. In addition we need to be aware that the surge of new regulations, legislation, guidance and systems does not become so restrictive that accommodation turns into a shadow of the institutions that we have fought so hard to close over recent years. This point was highlighted in the Learning Disability Taskforce Report (2004):

The Task Force is worried that some people with learning disabilities who have been happy where they live feel like their homes are turning into institutions because there are so many new rules to follow. (p. 73)

Housing will be revisited in Chapter 8.

Later life issues

Nowadays it is far more likely that people with learning disabilities, including those with ASDs, will have a longer and healthier life which then poses an increased problem for society. To be in a position to ensure effective provision is available for these people we must, as a society, move now to set in place those required services before it is too late.

For the majority of the population a time will occur when our parents pass away, but with the support of our friends, partner and children we have many reasons to continue a long and happy life. While some people with ASDs enter and maintain meaningful intimate relationships and have their own children the majority will not. Therefore, for this group, when parents have passed away there are fewer close relationships which link them to their home, background and culture. Some adults with ASDs will be living in homes based in a local community, but how well are they accepted into that community and how much support will they receive from the community members? Naturally some will have forged links with members of the local community but the majority will be excluded from the community they live among. If our friends, family and community give us a sense of belonging then we can see that for anyone with diminished social contacts they are more likely to be socially excluded.

For those adults with ASDs who live into old age, health problems are likely to arise more frequently (as they do for all of us) and interactions with health professionals in health centres, GP surgeries and hospitals will increase. Such appointments can cause many difficulties for those with ASDs who do not generally interact well with unfamiliar people and can find medical treatments and interventions very difficult to cope with. Special consideration needs to be given to this area not only now, but also more importantly in the future. Most importantly the professionals involved will need training to ensure they are knowledgeable of the difficulties experienced by adults with ASDs to ensure their difficulties are not compounded further.

Bigby (2005: 673) questions whether 'lifestyle support' should be considered for all adults with learning disabilities whereby:

new or specialised programmes should be designed for older people or whether they should utilise programmes for people with disabilities of all ages or for older people in the general community.

She goes on to offer strategic approaches to support such developments which could be:

... Incorporated into a variety of programme models:

- provision of choice and person-centred planning

- maintenance and strengthening of social networks

- support for participation in the community

- maintenance of skills

- opportunities for self-expression and sense of self

- promotion of health and a healthy lifestyle. (ibid.: 674)

It is clear that the government needs to act early to avoid problems in the future to ensure appropriate provision is in place for all adults with ASDs that will require it.

Impact on families

The preceding discussion of employment, housing and ageing are just three examples of significant issues that are likely to create a range of difficulties for the family members of adults with ASDs. These difficulties would include:

- accessing appropriate and useful information regarding the availability of services, funding and resources
- time, transport and finances to find the right accommodation
- accessing information about the quality of local residential services
- 'managing' health issues and treatment
- fighting to have their 'voices' heard
- work–life balance issues being changed
- isolation from friends
- the need to fight barriers and challenges they confront
- an understanding of how services work and how professionals work together
- exaggerated difficulties of their son/daughter at times of transition.

Summary

The impact of having a child with an ASD will have been considerable and will have placed long-term pressure on each and every family member. At the current time these pressures are unlikely to be relieved when their child reaches adulthood. The key issues raised in the Survey of Adults with Learning Difficulties in England 2003/4 (Internet 11) related to:

- social exclusion

- unemployment

- lack of socialising with friends and family

- bullying at school and abuse in adulthood

- being victims of crime

- little choice about accommodation

- lack of privacy

- lack of control over own spending

- unmet needs.

So clearly we can see that just about all the significant areas of an adult's life are negatively affected for those with ASDs which is a situation that must be addressed. Hopefully the introduction of legislation and guidance since the survey was completed will have already made a positive impact, but to achieve the government's aims as laid out in Valuing People (DoH, 2001b), we must ensure continued progress. Removing some of the pressures and barriers for adults with ASDs will, in turn, relieve the stresses for their parents, and this is what we must strive for.

Key issues

❖ The impact on family members will be cumulative throughout their child's childhood and adulthood.

❖ Professionals need to reflect on the impact on individual family members.

❖ Significant issues still affecting the lives of those with ASDs include housing, money, social exclusion, employment, having their voices heard and access to educational opportunities.

❖ Significant changes have been set in place by the government and these must be followed through to ensure continued progress.

Suggestions for discussion (professionals)

1. Consider an individual you are currently working with or have worked with in the past and reflect on your awareness of the impact on their family members over the years.

2. Make a list of ways in which you could further support the needs of family members.

3. Identify ways to make this happen.

Suggestions for discussion (parents)

1. Do you feel you are adequately supported by the professionals working with your son/daughter? If not think of ways in which this could improve. If your response is 'Yes' then think of ways of sharing this information with other parents.

2. Do you feel adequately informed regarding your son's/daughter's rights? If not how could you find out?

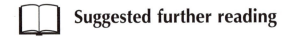 **Suggested further reading**

DoH (2001) *Valuing People: A New Strategy for Learning Disability in the 21st Century.* London: Stationery Office.

Howlin, P. (2004) *Autism and Aspergers Syndrome: Preparing for Adulthood.* 2nd edition. London: Routledge.

Loynes, F. (2001) *The Impact of Autism: A Report Compiled for the All Party Parliamentary Group on Autism.* London: APPGA.

6

Intervention programmes

This chapter explores:
➤ a range of intervention approaches;
➤ features of good practice;
➤ commonalities between effective practice in education, health and social care settings.

Introduction

As we have seen in earlier chapters the reality for adults with autism can be negative so we currently find ourselves in a situation where much more is known about ASDs, yet provision across education and care for adolescents and adults with ASDs may well be patchy. At times exemplary practice is evident but for the majority this is not the case. Many adolescents are attending schools, colleges and universities where staff have little knowledge of ASDs, while the majority of adults are either living at home or in residential care. If this is the current situation then clearly we are not addressing the needs of adolescents and adults with ASDs appropriately or effectively. In the worst situations those with ASDs are experiencing provision that at best offers some appropriate activities, but lack of knowledge about ASDs means that those responsible for their education and care are compounding the situation through the provision of inappropriate activities and/or inappropriate responses to the individual's ASD-specific behaviours.

Within home or care settings in many day centres around the country, basic skills, IT, literacy and numeracy, independence and other 'curriculum' areas are being developed, so clearly there is a strong 'education' focus in this aspect of care work. Likewise there is a strong element of 'care' to be found in education within pastoral work, citizenship and personal, social and health education (PSHE). So while historically we have pigeonholed education and care quite separately, we can see that in fact commonalities do exist. Appropriate intervention approaches will be explored in relation to the interactive nature of both education and care. The principles of effective provision are the same and will be built on our underpinning knowledge of ASDs as well as our knowledge of the individuals themselves that we are providing for in our settings. These factors are far more important than which professional discipline we work within or which approach we select.

A brief history of interventions

Back in the 1950s and 1960s autism was considered to be a form of schizophrenia and referrals were generally made to psychiatric specialists with drug treatment being the preferred option which was often administered in mental hospitals if the individual was deemed 'unmanageable' either in the community or within the home. Thus the intervention, in the light of today's considerably increased knowledge, would have been likely to be far from appropriate, with little reflection on the ASD needs of the individuals.

Once we had moved into the 1960s and beyond, as knowledge increased, behavioural approaches became more readily utilised to address the needs of adults and children with ASDs, but these were generally based on the operant conditioning theory that an individual demonstrates an unacceptable or negative behaviour and professionals need to change or eliminate that behaviour through the use of rewards. As Presland (1993: 127) outlined:

> A behavioural approach assumes that, if a problem behaviour occurs because of particular antecedents and consequences, it can be made to occur less by changing those conditions.

Such an approach would:

> ... be divided into stages based on the concepts described above. The most common sequence is as follows:

- Defining the problem

- Measuring the problem

- Determining existing antecedents and consequences for a problem behaviour

- Deciding what changes to make in antecedents and consequences

- Planning and implementing a programme

- Monitoring. (ibid.)

For many children, young people and adults this would be undertaken as a long-term inpatient, again often in mental institutions or special schools. This treatment would generally focus entirely on the elimination of unwanted and unacceptable behaviours such as violence and aggression, tantrums, self-harming and even rocking and hand flapping. Of course, we can now see that this type of treatment was totally inappropriate, but can hopefully appreciate that this was due to the limited understanding of ASD and the reasons behind such behaviours at that time. Positive rewards would be used to encourage positive behaviours, much as we do today, but negative behaviours were often greeted with punishments or even electric shock treatments (Howlin, 2004), an idea that will appear abhorrent to many readers.

During the 1970s, 1980s and 1990s texts to inform parents and professionals alike began to roll off the presses. Influential writers of the time included Frith, Howlin, Jordan, Lord, Rutter, Schopler and Mesibov and Wing. During this period treatments and interventions changed focus and early intervention became a key feature of the developing early years programme to ensure effective provision from the early years onwards to adulthood. The psychiatric approaches also diminished in favour of more individualised approaches responding to the known areas of difficulty for those with ASDs. Through this period, and to the present day, a multitude of specific approaches has emerged, some of which even claim to 'cure' autism. With such claims being made we can understand why parents could be tempted to invest much time and money in these schemes as the effects of ASDs on the family are considerable and long-term.

Many of the books and articles written relate more to the education of children with ASDs than relate to adults with ASDs, but the emerging information about adults often falling through the net of provision is creating increased interest in this area of work. As diagnosis has improved significantly over the years, allied with increased knowledge of ASDs, we are now experiencing times when more and more children are being diagnosed and progressing through to adulthood. Thus it has become more important than ever to establish appropriate approaches for adults with ASDs.

Early identification

There is now a wealth of evidence in support of early intervention, as concluded by Howlin (2004: 62):

> It is widely accepted that early intervention is vital in helping children with autism to develop essential skills in the earliest years, and in preventing the escalation of later behavioural difficulties.

Although this book relates to adolescents and adults with ASDs the impact of increased early diagnosis and appropriate intervention will be partly responsible for the current levels of ability of those adolescents and adults we are currently working with. If early identification took place, followed by effective provision throughout the early years and school years, then the adult is likely to be more able to cope with the world in which they find themselves. For those that have not experienced such provision their difficulties may have remained static or even deteriorated, and whatever their current level of functioning we will now be responsible for their education and care.

Over recent years much research has been undertaken in an attempt to confirm the effectiveness of early intervention but there is a lack of clear empirical evidence pointing to the success of early intervention programmes. This does not mean, however, that we should consider removing early diagnosis and intervention, which would be both foolish and short-sighted. We also need to remember that many adolescents will not have received an early diagnosis and late diagnosis is less common. It is accepted that appropriate strategies, based on in-depth knowledge of ASDs and the individual concerned, should be set in place whenever appropriate and regardless of age at diagnosis (or lack of diagnosis) and this is the key to effective provision. Just because ASD-specific strategies have not previously been put in place does not mean they should not be instigated now – in fact if the person has struggled to understand the world so far it is their right and our duty to provide strategies and support that will help to alleviate their difficulties. In my own experience there are educators and carers who try to reduce or eliminate the sometimes severe behavioural difficulties that can occur in adolescence and adulthood, but perhaps we should be taking stock of how and why these behaviours have developed in the first place to understand them more effectively.

Case Study 6.1 Joanne

Joanne is 14, has a diagnosis of ASD and attends a mainstream comprehensive school. She is sent to the head teacher at least three times each week for spitting at, swearing at and hitting out at her fellow pupils. The situation has been escalating and usually results in several other pupils becoming involved in the fighting. Currently she finds herself again in the head teacher's office being threatened with exclusion if she cannot learn to control her behaviour.

Joanne's main area of difficulty is social skills and social interactions and she desperately wants to be friends with a small group of her peers but does not understand how to establish and maintain friendships. Her attempts to be friendly and be accepted are perceived as blunt and overpowering by her peers and, due to Joanne's lack of understanding and awareness of how to behave in social situations, she tends to get angry, frustrated and anxious. This results in her outbursts of frustration which present as inappropriate and aggressive behaviours.

So how could the school attempt to support Joanne with her behaviour? With an understanding of ASDs a teacher could identify the cause of the outbursts and perhaps introduce social skills training into Joanne's timetable. If she was enabled and empowered to improve her social skills then the behaviours would be likely to diminish or even disappear. It is basically having the knowledge to identify the root cause of the outbursts and address that rather than simply address the outbursts which still leaves her a vulnerable, frustrated and anxious young lady who is likely to become a more regular visitor in the head teacher's office or even excluded from school.

Research supporting the use of specific intervention programmes with adults is very limited but if we understand the effects and impact of ASDS on the individual then we should be able to implement appropriate support if we can identify the aspect of ASD that is creating the difficult or unacceptable behaviours.

Specific approaches

There is currently a range of specific intervention approaches available to parents and professionals alike, some of which are meant to be used exclusively but others can be utilised as stand-alone strategies and are deemed examples of good practice. Many professionals, whatever their working situation, will select the most appropriate strategies to address the individual needs of those in their care, in an eclectic manner. I would argue that it is far more appropriate to begin with the individual and identify their strengths and weaknesses, likes and dislikes and specific ASD-related behaviours. Then appropriate strategies can be planned and implemented to address their specific – and individual – needs. Jones et al. (2001: 24) support this view, concluding that:

> Services and schools in the UK often use a number of different approaches, reflecting the diversity of children within the spectrum and the skills and areas of development which need to be addressed.

When considering specific approaches professionals and parents need to work together to ensure the most appropriate match between the approach and the individual's needs. Roberts (1999) offers a useful checklist before deciding on a specific approach which is adapted here for reflection:

1 Is the approach proven to be successful?

2 Is it possible to use this approach with this adult/child?

3 What are the likely long-term benefits?

4 Are there any short-term benefits?

5 What are the benefits for the family?

6 Is the approach lawful (relating to sanctions, punishments, etc.)?

7 How will progress be monitored?

8 Are people available to deliver the approach?

TEACCH

Standing for the Treatment and Education of Autistic Related Communication Handicapped Children the TEACCH programme was established in North Carolina in the 1960s and developed into a state-wide intervention approach for those with ASDs from early childhood through to adulthood. With the support of the families and their communities the TEACCH programme has grown to offer a range of supported employment schemes to enable those with ASDs to maintain secure employment within appropriate industries. Either living at home, independently or in supported accommodation, adults with ASDs can lead a satisfying and meaningful life within which they can achieve their maximum potential.

Implementation begins with a detailed assessment of the individual and then a tailor-made package of support will be devised, implemented and monitored. The key principles guiding the TEACCH programme are assessment of the individual's strengths and areas of deficit and the use of social skills training and structured teaching. Structured teaching revolves around a comprehensive understanding of the ways in which those with ASDs function and offers a clearer structure to avoid confusion, frustration and fear and to support future learning. The structures are:

1 Organising the physical environment to enable learning

2 Introducing schedules or timetables in an appropriate format

3 Introducing standardised working systems

4 Clear guidance to organise tasks.

Acknowledging that sensory difficulties can impede an individual's ability to focus and concentrate on specific tasks, whether it be listening or engaging with a task, the TEACCH system recommends separating areas of the room with dividers or storage units. This way the adolescent or adult will have a clearer understanding of what will be expected in each area which will help alleviate stress, uncertainty and anxiety. The individual timetable will empower the individual to follow their set order of tasks for the morning or day as they are followed in strict order. This again supports clarity of understanding and the reduction of any uncertainty when the individual knows what to do next and what will happen after that. Once seated in a 'working' area the individual will follow their learned left-to-right pattern of working – taking their task from the left-hand side of the area (perhaps in a named tray), completing the task and then placing it to the right, indicating the end of the task. Taking themselves back to their timetable will then clarify what they should do next and which area of the room to go to. Each task will have clear guidance or instructions or be familiar to the individual so again we see clarity of understanding as a key factor in creating increased independence and enabling learning.

While we do not have a comparable system in the UK there are many professionals (mainly educators) who have undergone TEACCH training in the UK and feel that the approach is the answer to resolve all the issues related to educating children and adolescents with ASDs when, in fact, a little knowledge can sometimes be detrimental for all involved. Having undergone the three-day Introduction to TEACCH training myself I remember coming away feeling that this was indeed the answer and that once I had reorganised my activity room and set up timetables and structured activities all would be well. Staff, children and parents would be less stressed and the children would be learning. On reflection, a key issue for me was that we would be teaching the children to function within a very prescribed environment and outside of school hours this environment would not exist, so were we in fact setting children up for increased anxiety in alternative environments? This issue has also been considered by Breakey in the context of FE (2006: 49):

> There is also a significant problem in that the structure offered by TEACCH effectively acts as a prop for the autistic person, without addressing cognitive processes. Without the support of the wider programme, there is a danger that when the structure is removed, the autistic person is left with no prop. This results in the wider criticism that the TEACCH programme is not one of education, but one of training, as it gives no responsibility, choice or control to the autistic person.

A further issue arises if an adolescent or adult has learnt within a TEACCH environment and is then moved to another part of the country or even locally to an establishment which does not utilise the approach. Whether TEACCH is being used or not professionals and parents should remember that: 'Whilst the TEACCH approach may be highly relevant to some, or even the majority with autism, it may not be appropriate for all' (Wall, 2004: 89), so the individuality of the student or client and their specific needs are again highlighted as of paramount importance.

Daily Life Therapy (Higashi)

This programme, originally created in Japan, focuses on physically demanding daily exercise regimes and a group working ethos. Its aim is to create the 'rhythm of life' for those with ASDs aged between three and 22 years of age. Roberts (1999: 23) states:

> The claim is that the rigorous use of daily group exercises reduces anxiety, increases stamina and allows a child to understand rhythm and routine. There is a strong academic emphasis and this promotes the pupils' potential for inclusion.

The DLT school offers residential and day facilities and the routines are also maintained within the residential setting throughout the waking hours. Currently there are schools in Boston (USA), Tokyo (Japan) and, more recently, in London. As no equivalent of the National Curriculum is followed then difficulties could arise when an adolescent returns to mainstream or special school that does not implement the programme. However, some advocates claim the results are very positive, with reduced anxieties and reduced inappropriate behaviours resulting from the renewed focus on exercise and routine, both of which offer structure to the individual. Another potential difficulty lies in DLT schools not using signing or augmented communication approaches for those with little or no language as all the instructions, directions and support are verbal which could pose potential difficulties.

ABA (Applied Behavioural Analysis)

NB: While the ABA approach usually relates more to younger children it is felt justified to outline the approach for information.

The ABA approach (often referred to as the Lovaas approach as it stemmed from the work of Lovaas in the 1970s) has its foundations in Skinner's and Pavlov's theories of behaviour. We are probably all familiar with Pavlov's work with dogs, wherein the importance of *antecedents, behaviours* and *consequences* (ABC of behaviour) were deemed crucial to changing behaviours. If the consequence is a positive experience or reward then the dog (or human being) is likely to repeat the behaviour, and it is this fundamental principle that lies at the root of the Lovaas approach. Lovaas worked with young, non-verbal children who had received a diagnosis of autism and the programme is delivered within the home. Trained ABA therapists will lead up to 40 hours per week of intensive behavioural therapy which it claims improves behaviour and can initiate the use of language. Some advocates claim remarkable success with children developing 'normal' skills and abilities by the time they reach seven, eight or nine years old.

In a basic example the young child would be seated at a small table opposite the therapist. If the task focus is on building three bricks into a tower, the therapist will demonstrate the task to the child, then push the bricks towards the child. If no response is forthcoming the therapist may place the child's hands on the bricks. If the child still fails to engage with the task the therapist will repeat the process until the child engages. If the child removes him/herself from the table they will be reseated. This process will continue over and over until engagement occurs. No matter how little effort is offered by the child they will be rewarded with either a small piece of food (e.g. a crisp) or toy to occupy themselves with momentarily. Then the next task will be introduced. Once progress is underway then the food or toy rewards would be replaced with praise, applause and smiles, which are more commonplace and acceptable. Over time, as the parents observe these sessions it is hoped they will begin to take over and lead some of the therapy sessions, thus reducing the need for the attendance of trained therapists so regularly.

Opponents to such a programme would argue that the young child with ASD does not want to interact with anyone and initially the insistence on being seated could result in considerable anxiety and upset for the child. In addition children with ASDs do not generally wish to engage in adult-led activities, preferring to remain within their own world of familiar and sometimes repetitive activities which offer security and comfort. One could also argue that to teach skills in such a 'robotic' manner is likely to result in the child not being able to complete the same task outside of the usual therapy environment and that the ability to transfer skills to other environments is essential for all children.

For some families the required levels of commitment, stamina and patience from themselves and their friends could rule out the ABA approach as a possibility for consideration. Yet those that have the commitment required would argue that the ability to start with very young children and be based at home place it as a favourable option that is likely, in their view, to reap many rewards.

Son Rise (options approach)

This approach was developed by the Kaufmans in America and was the result of their own work with their young son, Raun, who was diagnosed with autism at about 18 months of age. Now an adult, the Kaufmans claim he no longer demonstrates any aspects of autism to the extent that he no longer has autism and is therefore 'cured'. Through believing that their son had a lot to offer and that they should be more accepting of his 'autistic' world they began a process of interacting with him in the activities he chose, as opposed to imposing activities upon him. They imitated his play to indicate their acceptance of the way he was occupying himself. After a period of time their son began to acknowledge their presence more and more, so they were able to grasp opportunities to extend his play further and in a less stereotypical manner. All of this took place in a specially designed nursery/play room. After initial successes the Kaufmans recruited the support of their family and friends to enable the play sessions to run for the whole day, with the adults coming together frequently for evaluative sessions and future planning. The system, they claim, helps the child to learn what he wants to learn as opposed to what we feel they ought to learn, and as such is more successful than alternative approaches.

Due to the costs involved parents from the UK have often been prohibited from attending the intensive residential training at the Kaufman's centre, but those that have been able to afford it have had to set up their own designated play room before they travelled to begin their therapy immediately they returned. Videos, e-mails and phone calls can then be shared with the American centre to discuss difficulties, successes and future plans.

Again concerns spring to mind. If the child with an ASD is happy to remain in his/her own world then clearly this approach would be favourable. However, it limits the opportunities to develop social skills with other children, family and friends and to attempt the transference of skills into alternative environments. Yet again, proponents of this approach claim that children can develop purposeful speech and improved behaviours alongside a range of developmentally appropriate cognitive skills.

SPELL (National Autistic Society)

This system, developed by the NAS, is used throughout their own independent, boarding and day schools across the UK. The NAS (2001: 48) state the aim of their approach is:

> To provide a broad and balanced curriculum that takes account of the pupil's autism and learning needs and teaches independence and life-enhancing skills and experiences. Access to the National Curriculum is incorporated into individually designed programmes.

Every child and adolescent will be taught in small classes using structure, routine, consistency of approach and low levels of distraction to reduce anxieties and allow engagement. All staff will be trained in the approach so the whole school (and all staff, including non-teaching staff) will follow the principles and strategies outlined in the programme.

The name SPELL derives from the key elements within the programme:

Structure–which helps reduce anxiety and stress and creates security within the classroom environment.

Positive attitudes to success and expectations that are achievable and realistic yet still supporting development.

Empathy–through understanding the world and difficulties of the pupil with autism.

Low arousal–an environment which is free from too many distractions to enable the child to access the curriculum and achieve maximum learning.

Links–with parents, schools, the community and other professionals involved with the pupil and/or family.

(Adapted from Wall, 2004: 91)

The principles and delivery of this approach would be embedded within the NAS principles and understanding of all issues related to ASDs, which is clearly a major strength. In addition, transferable skills are taught and strong links with the home and family are maintained. Further credibility is offered as government Ofsted inspections undertake the quality assurance process within the schools and parents can therefore be assured of the effectiveness, running and management of the schools and the approaches used with their children.

Another aspect of NAS developments was the establishment of the Early Bird programme aimed at training parents to work with their pre-school children following the principles of increased understanding of autism, developing strategies to improve the child's communication and interaction, and learning to analyse the child's behaviours in a way to support the introduction of strategies to reduce the unacceptable behaviours.

Approaches to support communication difficulties – PECS (Picture Exchange Communication System)

Developed by Lori Frost and Andy Bondy in the 1980s the PECS system utilises the fact that people with autism are visual thinkers and need visual supports to develop new skills. It also focuses on the development of the fundamental principles of reciprocal communication that many of us take for granted, but is often lacking in people with ASDs. If you think back to any learning situation you have been involved in, be it at school, on a training course or watching a documentary, most of the information will be imparted verbally. Therefore in a world that predominantly communicates verbally it is essential to try and develop strategies to improve communication in those who have difficulties in this area, to enable increased participation within society.

PECS progresses through six phases from beginning to develop and understand the basic principles of communication between two people up to creating sentences, answering questions and developing the ability to comment on situations. Again, this approach is generally instigated with younger children but the benefits have remained clear: the person is enabled to develop increased independence as they can 'ask' for what they want, 'tell' how they are feeling and participate in conversations. Fears that the use of symbols on cards which are exchanged for desired objects or to convey meaning are likely to reduce the likelihood of speech developing have proved unfounded. In my own experience the use of picture cards has reduced stress and anxiety and poses fewer 'threats' than being confronted by someone who wishes to engage you in conversation. In this respect the desire or need to speak becomes less urgent and often with these pressures reduced speech does tend to develop along with the use of the picture symbols.

Approaches to support communication difficulties – Makaton

Makaton is a basic signing system whereby each sign has an accompanying line drawing to give pictorial support. Again this picks up on the need for individuals with ASDs to have visual strategies to support them. The signs are simple, and at the basic level can be understood by most people. I have seen children and non-verbal adolescents use Makaton very successfully with some taking their signs on small cards on a key clip attached to their belt or school bag for use whenever required to convey needs or desires or for adults to indicate what happens next or what they require the individual to do. In addition, when confronted with someone who does not understand the Makaton signs, the pictures can be used to help get meaning across. I have also seen Makaton used successfully in residential care homes with adults with ASDs and the fact that the individuals have a means of communicating and making choices offers increased independence and tends to reduce some of the undesirable behaviours that had occurred when they have previously not been understood or have not had their needs met.

Other approaches

As time moves on more and more approaches aimed at supporting those with ASDs are emerging. These include:

- facilitated communication
- Auditory Integration Training (AIT)
- sensory training
- ICT education and therapy
- play therapy

- drama therapy
- music therapy
- art therapy
- dance and drama therapy
- dietary and vitamin supplement therapies
- the Tomatis method
- social skills groups
- the Dolphin project
- hippotherapy (working with horses)
- massage therapy
- homeopathy

and the list goes on ...

Which approach do we use?

Bombarded with such a vast selection of possible approaches, how can parents or professionals be expected to select the most appropriate approach for the individual with ASD they are working with or caring for? Arguably I would recommend that we go back to basics and begin with the individual first and assess their needs fully before deciding on any approach or strategy to implement. Whatever strategies or approaches we put in place we must ensure we are taking into account the individual and their unique difficulties in a person-centred/client-focused manner. In addition we must involve the individual in our planning as we should not presume that as parents or professionals we 'know best'. This is only likely to result in less choice and independence for the individual and increased frustration and anxiety, resulting in more unacceptable outbursts of inappropriate behaviours. That which we have set out to diminish we have in fact promoted and encouraged. We cannot offer one approach for all those we meet with an ASD as this will not be meeting their needs appropriately and is unlikely to result in any measure of success. Rather we must explore and assess the individual and formulate our activity plans based on that knowledge and information, combined with our own knowledge and understanding of ASDs.

The National Centre for Autism Studies was commissioned to complete a literature review of autism by HM Inspectorate of Education, with the document being published in 2005 (Internet 10). The review examined a diverse range of intervention approaches and offered a range of perspectives on the effectiveness of each approach. Highlighting that there is often a lack of valid evidence to substantiate the effectiveness of any particular approach they identified that many reports of 'successes' are researched and written by individuals directly involved in the approach, thus registering the findings as biased and lacking validity. The report concluded that 'most approaches offer some evidence of positive and useful intervention results, [but] an eclectic model for supporting a person with autism is emerging' (Internet 10).

The following two chapters will explore the principles of effective provision within education and care settings for the individuals we are working with, but the key aspects of effective approaches can be summarised as:

- knowledgeable staff
- flexibility to work with individual needs
- regular observations to inform planning
- structured environments
- support for communication and social difficulties
- effective systems for working with other agencies
- working with and respecting the parents' perspective within an equal partnership and shared responsibility.

Summary

With a wealth of ideas and strategies readily available to us the skill is not necessarily to select the single approach to start using immediately but to explore the most appropriate techniques for the person we are seeking to support. It is unlikely that any single approach will be the panacea for all individuals with ASDs but some of their underlying principles can and will inform us of appropriate strategies to utilise, such as visual support, understanding ASDs and understanding why individuals sometimes behave inappropriately rather than trying to stop them from doing so. Our knowledge, of ASDs and the individual, are our strength and should be the focus for any planned interventions.

Key issues

❖ Our knowledge and understanding of ASDs and the individuals we work with will support our planning and the selection of approaches to be used.

❖ There is a range of approaches available but it is more appropriate to respond to individual needs as opposed to delivering a set programme.

❖ Many professionals will develop an eclectic approach using the proven principles of working with individuals with ASDs.

❖ Individuals with ASDs should be involved in decision-making processes.

Suggestions for discussion (professionals)

1. Discuss as a team the range of strategies that you incorporate in your working practice. Identify which aspects of ASDs they support most effectively and try to assess their success in the light of your experiences.

2. In small groups brainstorm one or two individuals you are working with. Outline their specific difficulties and describe how you are providing to meet their needs. As a group discuss ideas and potential strategies that could be employed for these individuals.

3. Consider all those who work in your setting (including cooks, caretakers, drivers, etc.) and explore how they can also adopt appropriate techniques to support individuals.

Suggestions for discussion (parents)

1. Consider the strategies you use at home that work successfully with your son/daughter. How is this information shared with their school/care setting? Could liaison between yourself and them be improved?

2. If you feel improvements could be made, discuss how you could implement changes.

 Suggested further reading

Breakey, C. (2006) *The Autism Spectrum and Further Education: A Guide to Good Practice*. London: Jessica Kingsley. (Chapter 2)

Hanbury, M. (2005) *Educating Children with Autistic Spectrum Disorders*. London: Paul Chapman. (Chapter 5)

Wall, K. (2004) *Autism and Early Years Practice*. London: Paul Chapman. (Chapter 5)

7

Appropriate provision in education

This chapter explores:
➤ current aspects of educational provision for students with ASDs;
➤ issues of inclusion and transition;
➤ key areas of ASD difficulty within an educational environment;
➤ effective strategies.

Introduction

Throughout the preceding chapters we have considered the characteristics of young people and adults with ASDs and reviewed the legislation surrounding their education and care. We have identified that the knowledge and skills of the professional involved is crucial to effective provision. Ultimately we found from several reports (Barnard et al., 2000, 2001, 2002; Broach et al., 2003) that in all aspects of life people with ASDs are still being excluded and this is simply not acceptable. Yet the government is stating that by 2025 the lives of all people with disabilities will be significantly improved. It is the right of every human being to be actively included in their communities (locally and nationally) and to be able to achieve all that they are capable of, but so often people with ASDs are not granted this right.

As we have seen previously, many young people with ASDs of school age have historically been placed in special schools but increased inclusion means more and more are now attending mainstream schools, FE colleges and HE colleges. Prospectuses are likely to indicate that young people with disabilities can be provided for but what issues will need to be addressed by the school staff to ensure this becomes a reality for all young people with ASDs?

Educational systems and processes

In Chapter 2 we explored the staged approach to provision incorporating School Action and School Action Plus whereby students experiencing difficulties and needing extra support are initially placed on School Action. The teacher responsible for making this decision will inform the special educational needs coordinator (SENCO) who will advise and support the teacher in providing appropriate provision in consultation with the student and his/her parents. The SEN Code of Practice informs us that:

> When a subject teacher, member of the pastoral team or the SENCO identifies a child with SEN they should provide interventions that are additional to or different from those provided as part of the school's usual differentiated curriculum offer and strategies (School Action). (DfES, 2001b: 68)

All information about the child will be collated (including any that would have been passed on from primary school) and individual education plans (IEPs) will be drawn up suggesting approaches to secure progress in the designated areas of learning. These will be reviewed regularly. All teaching staff, across subject areas, should be involved in this process. The SEN Code of Practice identifies the key components of an IEP as:

- The short-term targets set
- The teaching strategies to be used
- The provision to be used
- When the plan is to be reviewed
- Success and/or exit criteria
- Outcomes (to be recorded when IEP is reviewed). (DfES, 2001b: 70)

If the student does not make progress on School Action it could be agreed at a review meeting that outside professional expertise is needed to advise and support the staff as to how to move forwards. At this stage the student would be moved to School Action Plus in which the processes outlined previously for School Action would continue with the added involvement of external specialists. For young people with ASDs this could be the support of an educational psychologist (EP) or ASD specialist support teacher. For the minority of students who still fail to progress and are causing significant concern, the SENCO, parents and the student may decide it would be appropriate for the student to have a statutory assessment of their special needs which would culminate in the drawing up of a Statement of SEN. To enable this all the evidence from School Action and School Action Plus would be considered. The statement would specifically outline the child's difficulties and set down exactly what support is needed and how that will materialise. Throughout the whole educational system, working with other agencies, working closely with parents and effective practices are seen as critical aspects of successful provision. However, evidence suggests that securing a statement is often yet another battle for teachers and parents alike.

To support teachers and support staff working with children with SEN the DfES provided the SEN Toolkit and also issued their own guidance for supporting students with ASDs: *Autistic Spectrum Disorders: Good Practice Guidance* (DfES/DoH, 2002). The guidance states that:

> Meeting the diversity of needs of children within the autistic spectrum requires a diversity of provision, based on sound common principles. We believe that this is already happening in many areas. We are confident this guidance will provide an impetus to raising awareness and the standards of support for children with ASDs ... (DfES/DoH, 2002: 3)

The guidance goes on to outline the key areas of difficulty for students with an ASD and offers eight key principles to be followed:

- Knowledge and understanding of ASDs
- Early identification and intervention
- Policy and planning
- Family support and partnership
- Involvement of children
- Cooperation with other agencies
- Clear goals
- Monitoring, evaluation and research. (DfES/DoH, 2002: 15–18)

The fundamental principle within the guidance is the need for knowledge and understanding of ASDs by those involved with the young people, but is this the reality? Having been engaged with professionals in a range of training events I have been surprised (and disappointed) that it is generally only a minority that are even aware of this guidance information. It is not the professionals' fault, rather that the DfES guidance is simply not reaching the very people at the heart of educational delivery. In addition we repeatedly see reports that suggest that much more training in ASD-specific knowledge is essential for all those who will be in contact with people with ASDs as we all know that ignorance can compound their difficulties further, despite the best of intentions. Yet there still appear to be professionals in direct contact with people with ASDs that are seeking appropriate training. So a contradiction exists which must be resolved as a matter of urgency. If we are to promote such guidance documents then we must ensure that the right professionals have access to them as well as appropriate training at national level.

Sadly for young people with ASDs appropriate provision at secondary education level is less evident than in earlier phases of education. While there is a range of early years and primary schools that have communication or ASD support units and effective inclusion into the mainstream classrooms can be accommodated at least part-time, the availability of similar support at secondary level is comparatively sparse. Pressure from league tables for schools to produce higher academic results and outcomes can also compound the availability of ASD-appropriate support systems. Perhaps the most significant problem lies in the lack of teacher understanding of ASDs which is crucial to effective support. Howlin (2004: 182) supports this view: 'Specialist training is vital in helping teachers to identify and understand pupils with autism.'

For parents of adolescents with ASDs the NAS has published a very useful and accessible guide to the current systems in the UK for children with ASDs (Waterhouse et al., 2006).

Issues of inclusion

The SENDA (DfES, 2001) promoted increased inclusion for students with special needs in mainstream provision and this was further supported in the DfES document *Inclusive Schooling: Children with Special Educational Needs* which stated that:

> The Act seeks to enable more pupils who have special educational needs to be included successfully within mainstream education. This clearly signals that where parents want a mainstream education for their child everything possible should be done to provide it. Equally, where parents want a special school place their wishes should be listened to and taken into account. (DfES, 2001c: 1)

So what constitutes effective inclusion? Inclusion can only be deemed successful if children and young people, with or without disabilities, are educated together in their local mainstream provision and all are achieving to their maximum potential. Yet this is unlikely to simply happen, as the school and individual staff must support full inclusion and ensure their own practices support success for all children and young people. For young people with ASDs this will mean that all staff will need to be knowledgeable about ASDs and their effects plus the most effective strategies to support pupils' needs.

As an example we can consider the actual delivery of the curriculum. In secondary school, college and university, lessons and lectures are predominantly delivered verbally and the teacher stands at the front and passes on the knowledge needed to the students. This may be supported by the use of written work, case studies, discussions, experiments, video materials, books and ICT. For students with ASDs verbal communication invariably presents significant difficulties so immediately we have a problem. For such students to be successful we need to develop alternative learning and teaching approaches to ensure they have equal access to the curriculum being offered.

In 2004 the government published *Removing Barriers to Achievement: The Government's Strategy for SEN* (DfES, 2004b) outlining their stance on the future of SEN provision. Eleven SEN Regional Partnerships in England were established to explore and support increased inclusion with a focus on SEN practices. Their brief was to develop and support inclusive practices, to support improved inter-agency working and to improve the efficiency of services. While all these principles and intentions are admirable it could be argued that without significant funding and training of all those involved in providing education many young people with ASDs will still be failing within our education system. The

2004 SEN strategy emerged from the Every Child Matters agenda working to ensure improved outcomes for all children across the country, but in 2006, four of the country's most prominent children's organisations formed an alliance entitled 'Every Disabled Child Matters', claiming that the Every Child Matters agenda will fail children with disabilities. So has the government got it right? Arguably not, as the DfES implemented a policy review of the provision for children with disabilities which 'highlights a gap between need and provision of services for disabled children' (Internet 16).

For young people with ASDs the NAS 2006 campaign 'Make School Make Sense' adds further issues to the debate (Batten et al., 2006) producing some damning evidence from the families of children and young people with ASDs, including:

- 66% of parents said their choice of school was limited by a lack of appropriate placements for children with autism in their local area.
- Only 30% of parents of children in mainstream education are satisfied with the level of understanding of autism across the school.
- … 23% of parents are dissatisfied with SENCOs' level of understanding of autism.
- Over 40% of children with autism have been bullied.
- 1 in 5 children with autism has been excluded and 67% of these have been excluded more than once.
- Only 53% of young people aged 14–19 years have transition plans, falling to 34% of students in mainstream schools. (Batten et al., 2006: 3)

The report makes a range of recommendations and offers examples of good practice but focuses key demands on three areas:

- The right school for every child
- The right training for every teacher
- The right approach in every school. (Batten et al., 2006: 3)

The evidence within the report, along with that from other research and information on education for children and young people with ASDs makes it clear that children with ASDs are currently being failed by the system – it is not the children and young people that are failing. Current generic government initiatives and strategies for children and young people with disabilities cannot succeed for those with ASDs unless the NAS campaign demands are listened to and acted upon.

The move to increased inclusion in education is to be commended and should remain our ultimate goal. However, the current rapid expansion in inclusion without appropriate training and funding could be seen as an inappropriate and overzealous attempt to create the ideal. Full and effective inclusion is a long-term process that cannot be hurried; it is a process that whole schools need to adopt fully and work to develop over a period of time. When staff feel their school can actively accommodate the needs of any child who may walk through their doors then they may be nearer the goal. For the time being training in inclusive practices should be initiated at national level before any more special schools are closed down and before any more children and young people with ASDs are being negatively affected by their current education provider, and thus their government. The House of Commons Select Committee report (2006) summarises their own view of the education system for children:

> Children with Autistic Spectrum Disorder (ASD) and social, emotional or behavioural difficulties (SEBD) provide an excellent example of where the old Warnock framework is out of date and where significant cracks exist in the system to the detriment of those who fall between them. Far more important, however, is the frustration and upset caused to parents and families by the failure of the system to meet the needs of these children. This needs most urgent resolution. (House of Commons, 2006: 18)

Transition issues

Points of transition can be notoriously difficult for those with ASDs as sameness and familiarity are preferred states. The move from the smaller and often more well known primary school where most lessons are led by the same teacher in the same classroom is likely to seem a world apart from the systems met in most secondary schools. Different teachers for different subjects, different rooms requiring moving around the building many times each day, the perceived (but not taught) notion of becoming a more 'independent learner' and the sheer numbers of people in the building can cause any child difficulties. For the child with ASDs these difficulties are likely to be multiplied in intensity many times. Thus any period of transition needs careful planning and coordination to be successful. Yet the NAS report (2004) highlighted that 'more than half of parents of 11–16 year olds are not aware of the 14+ transition review and what that review would mean for their child' (NAS, 2004: 1). An additional finding was that unless parents are prepared to fight for what their child needs it will not, necessarily, be offered automatically. So clearly the reality is that those young people with ASDs are not provided for appropriately at this crucial time.

When the young person in secondary school approaches the age of 16 they may be considering a move either to sixth form studies, to an FE college or out into the world of work. This particular period of transition, from child to adult services, is likely to be the most daunting of all for people with ASDs so again demands careful and sensitive planning. A transition plan will be essential with information from all parties involved informing the decisions being made, including the student and his/her parents. The Valuing People strategy stated that:

Disabled young people and their families often find the transition to adult-hood both stressful and difficult. For many there has been a lack of coordination between the relevant agencies and little involvement from the young person. (DoH, 2001b: 41)

The 14–19 Education and Skills White Paper (DfES, 2005b) was expected to address many significant barriers for young people with learning disabilities but the final proposals were not as forward-thinking as had been hoped for. For students with low academic achievement the proposals suggest a move to more qualifications, greater focus on key skills of numeracy and literacy, improvements to the transition period planning and increased employment opportunities.

The Connexions service has also undergone recent changes but still exists to provide services for all young people aged 13–19, and for those with disabilities this can be extended until aged 25. The Connexions personal advisers work with young people from an early stage so as to lead the transition planning, taking into account all relevant information from all parties. Ramjhun (2002: 79) stated that the Connexions service

> has the task of working with schools to prepare, monitor and implement the Transition Plan. This service is expected to ensure that a team of personal advisers are working with young people in order to help them progress into training, employment or some form of learning, by removing barriers to their participation.

Transition planning meetings should be established and participants should act as advocates and advisers to the students to ensure the student's own views are considered and that all professionals involved can support the student towards their chosen pathway. This will be crucial for students with ASDs but will clearly depend on the personal adviser's knowledge and understanding of ASDs and the issues this will raise for the student in their chosen pathway. The adviser could work to ensure that wherever the student chooses to move to, employment or further education, all appropriate support is available and in place before the student arrives. In addition they can ensure that all personnel involved after the transition are aware of the individual's specific difficulties. Personal advisers will work across professional boundaries so can become involved with health and social care professionals regarding individual issues relating to housing and health needs as required. Useful advice for supporting the transition from school to post-school provision or employment is offered in the DfES guidance document (2002b).

Many schools offer more vocational courses than ever before to give realistic options to those that are not pure 'academics'. For many people with disabilities, and more specifically those with ASDs, the opportunities to undertake work experience while at school will be both a desire and a right. Key skills which are transferable to the workplace or to further education will be essential to support success for young people with ASDs. While studying their curriculum-based subjects these students will also need ongoing training in social skills and communication as these are two key areas of difficulty that will impact significantly on all aspects of their adult life. Students with ASDs are also likely to need additional support in exam preparation as these can be particularly difficult and somewhat unnatural times. An examination hall running under examination conditions is stressful enough for any of us but for those with ASDs it is likely to present additional and significant challenges.

When a young person is wishing to enter a new educational establishment such as sixth form college, FE college or HE institution there needs to be clear and effective planning which is likely to include the following:

- support over decisions regarding choice of establishment
- initial visit(s) to familiarise
- support to understand and undertake the application process
- a meeting with the Disability Officer to establish the amount and type of support available
- visits to accommodation blocks if the student will be living in
- preparation and support for the interview process
- preparation regarding self-help and self-management
- meetings with subject tutors and personal tutors.

The National Association of Disability Practitioners is the 'professional organisation for disability and support staff in further and higher education' (Internet 17). It has a useful website containing a list of all FE and HE institutions which are members of the organisation, which could be used as a search tool to find an appropriate and accommodating future educational establishment for a young adult with an ASD.

Specific issues for students with ASDs

In Chapter 4 we unravelled the complexities of ASDs, noting that individuals would vary in the range and type of difficulties they experience. Fundamental to our ability to provide effective educational support will be our knowledge of the key areas of difficulty that were considered in some depth in the earlier chapter:

- social interaction
- social communication
- imagination.

With our knowledge of these three key areas of difficulty and the effects on individuals we need to be able to explore appropriate responses to teaching approaches and support. To accommodate the individuality of people with ASDs perhaps the most useful tool we will have is our knowledge and flexibility.

A common aspect of everyday teenage life, and thus school life, is that of being accepted by your peers. Peer pressure is arguably strongest for adolescents and it is common for teenagers to want to be one of the 'in-crowd'. This is likely to affect the way they speak, show respect, dress and behave. For teenagers with ASDs, who may appear to behave differently, this can be very difficult. They themselves may have no desire to be a part of the accepted teenage groupings but for others acceptance may be of paramount importance and being unable to fit in may become intolerable, resulting in outbursts of unacceptable behaviour or depression. Being unable to interact socially in an acceptable manner may be a significant problem and this would be partly due to the individual's inability to use their senses in a multi-functional manner. Engaging in a conversation while also listening to the conversation of someone behind you may be impossible, as will the inability to appreciate and interpret the nuances of teenage body language and facial gestures, yet both of these would be an integral part of socialising with the group. Donna Williams (1996, 1998a, 1998b) talks of this when describing her own ASD difficulties when growing up and there are other examples showing adolescents in typical social situations that present them with considerable challenges. Such instances can create considerable anxiety and frustration for the individual which is likely to result in behaviour which could be perceived as odd or bizarre to the peer group. At an autism conference I attended a couple of years ago there was an adult with an ASD who persistently interrupted the key speakers as if they were holding a one-to-one conversation. He was oblivious of the other 500 people in the room and was unaware that his behaviour was not appropriate. Thankfully this occurred in a supportive environment, but had it occurred in a cinema, theatre, classroom or lecture theatre it could have resulted in a range of negative outcomes such as bullying, personal comments, annoyance of peer group/audience and/or exclusion from the group. As the individual is unable to grasp the socially acceptable rules of behaviour in such situations, these skills need to be taught. A range of typical areas of difficulty have been recorded by adults with ASDs such as Grandin (1995), Williams (1992, 1996, 1998a, 1998b) and Lawson (2000, 2002) and give professionals and parents a personal insight into issues that may occur within their own situations.

Key areas of difficulty within an education environment

Each individual will be affected by their ASD in a unique and individual way and the role of professionals, in partnership with parents and the student, will be to ensure that all areas of difficulty are addressed so the needs of the individual can be met appropriately. However, there are some common areas of difficulty:

Difficulties in social interaction

- Enjoyment within social situations but an inability to initiate and/or maintain social contact.
- Conversely the individual may prefer to remain outside of social situations and appears rude although this is simply to avoid the problems he/she knows social situations can create.

- Inability to appreciate accepted rules of social contact, e.g. knowing when touching or intrusion into personal space is appropriate or not.

- Inappropriate or overly formal approaches to people, e.g. greeting everyone with a handshake and learnt phrases such as: 'Hello, my name is Andrew. What is your name?' which would clearly not be appropriate when arriving at a cash desk in a busy supermarket.

Difficulties in language and communication

- Individuals will range in their abilities to communicate verbally, from no speech to those with proficient levels of verbal language, although the latter may have difficulties in using their language appropriately.

- Literal understanding of language so the idioms we commonly use are likely to result in confusion. For example, 'Pull your socks up!' to most people means 'do better' but to the individual with an ASD it is likely to mean 'pull your socks up'. Imagine how confusing this would be if, as a teenage girl, you are wearing tights.

- Lack of ability to understand and interpret facial expressions, body language, gestures and/or tone of voice.

- Inability to act appropriately in a classroom, such as shouting out or calling out answers when everyone else knows it is expected that you raise your hand and wait to be asked to answer.

- Problems with the rules of social communication and thus conversation, such as not knowing when it is appropriate to enter a conversation or, being unaware that you should wait for someone to finish what they are saying before you speak.

Difficulties in the area of imagination

- Resorting to stereotypical behaviour which may be seen as odd or bizarre, such as rocking, making noises, self-biting, spinning, walking on tiptoes, covering eyes and/or ears.

- Problems with organisation (fundamental to secondary school existence) so not having the right materials on the right day or in the right lesson.

- Difficulties in unexpected changes to routine. For example, if Monday morning brings double maths followed by geography, then any changes, say for a fire drill or timetable swop, can result in extreme anxiety and confusion.

- Having narrow interests and expecting others to share in them, e.g. talking about the history of steam trains for periods of time and not realising that the listener(s) are bored and irritated.

- Repetitive routines such as organising their rucksack in a very specific way so if a lesson overruns they may be unable to get packed away quickly.

- Difficulties with planning their life, clearly having implications in secondary schools, FE or HE, when timetabling is fundamental and the workload needs to be managed.
- Having limited or no understanding of their impact on others.
- Difficulties following instructions or lengthy instructions.

Other common difficulties of ASDs

- Sensory difficulties with regard to touch, smell, taste, auditory and visual. For example, noise at lesson changeover time when corridors are bustling could be very difficult, as can smells in changing rooms and the dining room, music lessons, assembly.
- Speaking out of turn, upsetting others.
- Anxiety and confusion in unstructured areas such as playing fields, the playground, the dining hall, corridors.
- Limited concentration and attention span.
- Poor coordination which can result in poor handwriting. In addition they may see the need to finish set coursework at home but not see the need for it to be well presented.
- Appearing clumsy through poor gross motor problems.
- Need for visual cues and visual support systems.

Key issues for professionals in education settings

Once knowledge of the difficulties for students with ASDs has been secured professionals need to be aware of some fundamental issues that will require specific attention in their planning and organisation. These include:

- responses to inappropriate behaviours demonstrated
- classroom organisation and structure
- presentation of lessons and course materials to accommodate needs
- support during unstructured periods
- time out space or quiet space which can be accessed by the student in times of particular anxiety
- ways to increase the organisational skills of the student
- support during times of change, planned or otherwise
- support to develop the student's social communication and social interaction skills
- social skills training
- support for difficulties with stereotypical behaviours.

The difficulties for young people in secondary schools, FE or HE are clearly considerable, and without professionals who understand these specific difficulties well and who also know how to plan to accommodate needs, educational experiences can be dire. Howlin (2004: 179) confirms this view suggesting that:

> Others describe an almost total lack of understanding of their educational, social or behavioural needs. Occasionally the situation can be transformed by a sympathetic teacher … However, such opportunities seem to be due more often to chance than to appropriate educational planning, and all too many pupils with autism in mainstream school struggle through miserably; unsupported, misunderstood and often mistreated.

Other reports such as those published by the NAS support the need for knowledgeable teachers who are able to accommodate the needs of students with ASDs, with SENCOs (in secondary schools) and Disability Officers (in FE and HE) being crucial to successful outcomes. Chapter 5 indicated some of the key issues in education for students with ASDs.

Appropriate strategies

The first and most essential element of appropriate provision is knowledgeable staff and I make no apologies for raising this issue again and again throughout this book. It is the one, single, most powerful area that needs immediate attention at national level. Once this has been established we need to focus on the need for structure within the classroom environment, timetable arrangements, dealing with planned or unexpected change and flexibility of teaching approaches. Whatever strategies are introduced it is likely there will be additional requirements placed on staff; however, in time it would be hoped that the level of support would be reduced as progress is made, allowing the student greater independence. If the student has one-to-one support, either part-time or full-time, then it could be part of their responsibility to ensure these tasks are completed satisfactorily.

The layout and structure of the classroom itself can make life more difficult or easier for students with ASDs. Visual stimulation can be overpowering so displays and bright lights should be avoided if possible. Over-stimulation can also affect the student's ability to concentrate on tasks so simply by moving their desk or table to a quieter area of the room which is devoid of visual stimulation (not in front of a window or colourful display for example) can make a significant difference to their learning outcomes. If this is assisted by a visual summary of what they are expected to complete during this time they will be further supported and less anxious as the parameters are clear. A list of materials (written or visual) needed for the task will also enable the student to get organised quicker and feel less anxious.

To enable increased organisational skills and therefore reduce the occurrence of not being prepared for lessons, timetable lists could be accompanied by lists of essential materials for each lesson to immediately alleviate a range of common difficulties. A duplicate list could be placed on a notice board at home to reduce tensions there and to enable family members to offer support. Similarly, visual or written instructions can be provided to ensure the student can navigate around the building, particularly in the early days. It may also be possible to suggest the less obvious routes to avoid the crush and visual/auditory difficulties found in the corridors at lesson changeover times. Alternatively the student could be allowed to leave a lesson a few minutes before the end to reduce stress levels when moving to the next room.

During unstructured times the student with an ASD needs support to reduce anxieties and confusion so it could be that a quiet area for them to eat lunch and spend lunch and break times is offered. Some students with ASDs may prefer to spend free time on the computer, in the library or completing homework as free times are simply too stressful to cope with. For those who find these times less daunting it may be that they are assigned to an older pupil, member of their peer group or a member of staff who will act as a mentor and to whom they can go if difficulties arise. Whichever approach is decided upon staff must be aware of the potential for the student to be made fun of or bullied so systems should be in place to eliminate this. The ASD student may not realise whether his/her peers are laughing at him or socialising with him, so staff must be able to monitor this. Special arrangements may need to be considered for physical education lessons as they can often cause problems for those with ASDs. Flexibility will be the key with an ability to respond individually to students with ASDs and respond directly to the individual needs of each.

Homework or private study can themselves present additional problems beyond ensuring they take the right books and materials home as they may not be able to remember by the time they get home what homework was set. Simply photocopying this or writing it down for the student, say in a homework diary, could support this quite easily.

Social skills training will be needed for many young people with ASDs, as well as for many who do not have ASDs, to improve their social communication and social interaction skills. This will need to be assigned specific timetable slots to ensure success. Carol Gray has written much about social skills training and produced resources and materials to be used so it would be useful for staff to access these if unfamiliar with this area of work (Internet 18). In addition the student could be introduced to 'controlled' social situations within the school such as a chess club or computer club, as this would maintain their interest as well as offer social situations which could be a part of their social skills training.

Unexpected change is another area of focus for staff and if we reflect on a typical day in a secondary school, FE college or HE institution, we will see the student meets a considerable number of staff: individual teachers, the head teacher, dinner staff and support staff. This is routine for the student but when one of them is absent or there is a change in the timetable then anxieties are likely to rise. Students should have the opportunity for a more detailed explanation in a quiet environment, where support can be offered. Dealing with change could also be an aspect of the student's social skills training programme. If a student has a one-to-one support worker and/or a buddy mentor to support them through the academic day then if they are absent through illness the student will again need support to deal with this unexpected change.

As can be seen from the strategies suggested none of them requires specialist materials or are too complex to be implemented in any educational setting, they just require awareness of the difficulties and a flexible approach to finding ways to overcome them. The skills of the staff will be paramount. What is the point in insisting an adolescent with an ASD has to join in team games when they are unlikely to be wanted on anyone's team as they find it difficult to be a team player or to follow instructions? The benefits to the child are virtually nil but the potential negative effects can be considerable. With flexibility the student could be given a separate physical task to complete, or be allowed to attend another lesson or spend time with his one-to-one support worker. That way everyone benefits.

Staff must also be aware of the potential of the sensory difficulties the student with ASDs may experience as these can have a far reaching effect. Anyone that has been present in a school dining hall can probably recall the level of noise from talking to the clatter of cutlery and crockery, the smells and the visual sensations of the arrays of food. Combine this with a requirement to stand in an orderly queue among chatty peers who may well jostle each other in jest and we can appreciate that for the student with an ASD this could be a very difficult situation. Alternative arrangements may be required or at the very least some support should be given to the student.

The curriculum itself may also need adapting in light of the individual's needs as there is little point in insisting on a curriculum which offers little gain to any student. Within secondary schools the National Curriculum is followed, but the student can be supported to make appropriate decisions when it comes to options throughout their time there. In FE or HE the student is likely to self-select courses studied, with or without help in the decision-making, so there are likely to be fewer problems. Independence skills and social skills are arguably the most crucial skills to develop for all students with ASD and these must take into account the individual difficulties of each and every student.

Summary

For the student with an ASD in secondary school, FE or HE the difficulties experienced can be considerable and as we have noted previously the numbers of students with ASDs being excluded from education is greater than that of the general school population (Batten et al., 2006). Clearly education is not currently responding well to such students. Once staff are aware of the effects of ASDs on students and how they can develop their teaching and learning strategies to accommodate these needs then we may see further progress. Of course there are some schools and colleges that provide admirably for students with ASDs, but for the majority this is simply not the case. We are currently failing students, especially in secondary schools, and issues of training, funding and resources (human, time and materials) must be addressed at national level to ensure that we are 'valuing' those with ASDs within the philosophy of the *Valuing People with Learning Disabilities in the 21st Century document* (DoH, 2001b), which was published by the government and is now guiding working practices. We should always remember that our knowledge and flexibility will empower us as professionals to empower those students we work with.

Key issues

❖ Professionals' knowledge and understanding of ASDs and the individuals we work with will support person-centred planning and the selection of approaches to be used.
❖ Periods of transition will require thorough planning and appropriate support for the individual.
❖ The individual's views must be taken into account.
❖ Barriers to improvements must be identified and addressed.

Suggestions for discussion (professionals)

1. Assess the staff ASD training needs through questionnaires to the staff (teaching and non-teaching), the parents of students with ASDs and the students themselves asking their views.

2. Act upon the findings.

3. Ensure all members of the school, college or university staff have knowledge of appropriate strategies to implement and have the means to implement them.

Suggestions for discussion (parents)

1. Ensure the school, college or university is aware of any strategies that you have employed successfully at home that could be adopted in the school.

2. Ask to be involved in meetings relating to improvements for students with ASDs.

3. Inform the school, college or university of any resources they could access that you have found useful.

Suggested further reading

DfES (2002a) *Autistic Spectrum Disorders: Good Practice Guidance.* Nottingham: DfES.

Howlin, P. (2004) *Autism and Aspergers Syndrome: Preparing for Adulthood.* 2nd edition. London: Routledge.

Mesibov, G. and Howley, M. (2003) *Accessing the Curriculum for Pupils with Autistic Spectrum Disorders.* London: David Fulton.

Plimley, L. and Bowen, M. (2006) *Autistic Spectrum Disorders in the Secondary School.* London: Paul Chapman.

Appropriate provision in care settings

This chapter explores:
➤ current aspects of care provision for adults with ASDs;
➤ key issues for adults with ASDs;
➤ key areas of ASD difficulty within a care setting;
➤ effective strategies.

Introduction

Provision in care settings will automatically involve issues relating to housing, employment, leisure and health and we are currently seeing major changes at national level as a result of many reports and government initiatives identifying specific areas requiring improvement. The overarching aim is to empower adults with learning difficulties to have a greater say over the provision they engage with and to improve every aspect of their life to ensure they have rights, choices and access to healthcare and are included in their communities and wider society. At all stages provision will be governed by current legislation but while we have seen in Chapter 3 the force of change there are still major issues to be addressed to ensure all adults with ASDs are provided with appropriate support and opportunities to achieve their full potential.

Outcomes from many government reports indicated the need for a radical shake up of provision and the resulting legislation started with the Care Standards Act of 2000 which came from the *Modernising Social Services* White Paper. The aim was to improve standards, improve the quality of provision, reduce or eliminate existing inequalities and provide services that were easier to access and use. Other areas of focus were:

... the establishment of the following:

• An Independent National Care Standards Commission to regulate all care homes, private and voluntary healthcare, and a range of social care services in accordance with national minimum standards

- A General Social Care Council to raise professional and training standards for the million strong social care workforce
- The Training Organisation for Social Services, to improve both the quality and quantity of practice learning opportunities for social work students
- The Social Care Institute for Excellence, to act as a knowledge base and to promote best practice in social care services.   (Internet 7)

Clearly the effects of such radical changes will take time to become evident but it can be seen that considerable steps are being taken to improve services for all adults who need support. So parents of adults with an ASD should hopefully feel more assured of higher quality provision within all settings in the future. Many of the changes since 2000 emerged from the Valuing People strategy of 2001 (DoH, 2001b), identifying existing challenges and barriers for children and adults with learning disabilities and also outlining key areas for change and improvement:

- transitions into adult life
- person centred planning
- increased choice and control
- supporting carers
- improving health
- housing
- fulfilling lives
- employment
- quality services
- improved partnership working across professions and agencies.

Previously mentioned reports (Barnard et al., 2001; Harker and King, 2004; Loynes, 2001a) have each indicated to us key problem areas for adults with ASDs and illustrated the bleak reality for many. In 2006 the DoH published their report *Better Services for People with Autistic Spectrum Disorders* which is currently the most recent document – and arguably one of the first – to address issues for adults with ASDs as previously they were incorporated within the generic term of learning difficulties. The very individual and specific nature of ASDs was not represented in previous documentation and as a result adults with ASDs often 'fell through the net' between learning disability services and mental health provision. The new direction is hopefully changing this as it should ensure adults are involved in decision-making as well as aiming to improve the range and quality of services.

Care systems and processes

The current situation offers a range of services to adults with ASDs and we are moving away from a system in which provision would be decided on a diagnostic label such as 'learning disability'. The focus now is firmly on the individual difficulties of the adult with professionals working towards greater inclusion in society. Historically parents have reported on their long battles with systems and procedures to gain access for appropriate services for their adult child and significant improvements are well overdue. The appropriateness of services offered will be crucial to the future life of the adult with an ASD as they will affect well-being, happiness, independence, security and peace of mind for parents and carers. For this reason assessments of need should be undertaken by experienced professionals with knowledge of ASDs. Baworowski (2002: 29) retold his own battles when trying to secure day care provision for his 20-year-old son:

> It took about 16 months, the involvement of our MP and councillors, the best part of 200 letters and reports by various individuals (including the recommendation of some ten medical and educational professionals supporting us), a detour to the High Court and all three stages of social services' statutory complaints procedure to achieve the result.

Thankfully the intended outcome was achieved but no parents should have to engage in this level of intense argument with authorities to secure provision their son or daughter is entitled to. What should be remembered is that not all parents have the means, ability or desire to enter such a long-term battle for provision. Many parents of adults with ASDs will be well informed about ASDs, the range of provision that should be available and their own and their child's rights, but there are also others who take the provision that is offered and are relatively happy to 'accept their lot', assuming that if they were entitled to anything else they would have been informed. Hopefully current changes will relegate such instances to history and empower all parents and their adult children with ASDs.

Transition issues

Current policies have identified the need for thorough transition planning for all those with disabilities but the DoH publication (2006) focuses specifically on adults with ASDs and identifies the following:

- One single adult should lead the process to eliminate too many personnel confusing the adult and causing distress.
- Information should be available in good time for the adult and their family to make effective and informed decisions.
- Understand the adult's need for continuity, sameness and routine.
- Begin the process at age 14 years.

The transition from children's services to adult services will require careful planning for all adults with an ASD as it can be a stressful and difficult time with many changes occurring. In the past, evidence has suggested that lack of effective coordination between the supporting agencies involved has resulted in low-quality care plans and subsequent provision. Transition planning should also ensure continuity of care and support and enable the young adult to have every possible opportunity made available to them to ensure they lead fulfilling and happy lives and reach their full potential.

The Connexions service for all 13-19 year olds has been extended so that those with disabilities can remain supported by their Connexions advisor until the age of 25. Detailed reviews will be held regularly but with greater emphasis at the time of transition than at any other time. The Connexions advisor will also liaise with all other relevant agencies and professionals, such as social services and/or health services.

Care plans

Fair Access to Care Services: Guidance on Eligibility Criteria for Adult Social Care (Internet 19) was implemented by 2003 across the country to help local authorities with the eligibility criteria for needing support and therefore a care plan. 'The framework is based on individuals' needs and associated risks of independence, and includes four eligibility bands – critical, substantial, moderate and low' (ibid.).

Many adults with ASDs will be in need of some level of support throughout their adult lives. Depending on the individual a wide range of caring options needs to be readily available and accessible to ensure every adult can be accommodated appropriately. A full and detailed care assessment should be carried out covering every aspect of the individual's life to inform the provision offered. The assessment should address the following areas:

- housing and accommodation (including respite care if appropriate)
- health needs
- employment
- education
- social needs and leisure activities.

The voices of parents and the adults themselves must be integral to the assessment.

A health and social care assessment is usually undertaken by the local social services department whereby every aspect of the individual's life should be explored, with the adult's own views being fundamental to discussions. Any areas of need and support will be identified within a care plan and links made to relevant professionals for further action. Care plans will be reviewed regularly as needs are likely to change over time. A 'package' of support may be defined which could include a range of services from both the statutory and independent sectors. Advice on benefits and direct payments and how to apply will also be discussed with support being offered if needed. Within the direct payment scheme funding will be paid directly to the adult with an ASD (or their parent/carer as appropriate) to be used to access and pay for their own identified package of support. For example, the adult may wish to participate in horse riding regularly and this may not be provided by the local authority, but this could be secured through an independent organisation and paid for from the direct payment funding. The support offered could include care within the home, supported living arrangements, residential care, specialist equipment and/or access to day centre provision in the locality.

All registered services available now have to comply with the National Minimum Standards and will be subject to inspections by the CSCI who also inspect local social services provision. Areas inspected will include health and safety, access facilities, education and employment opportunities offered, quality of furnishings and fittings and personal care.

Housing and accommodation

Social care covers provision by local authorities as well as the independent sector and provides a range of accommodation options depending on individual circumstances, but including home care, day centres, supported living, independent living, residential care homes and nursing homes. Due to the lack of state residential homes in the past private organisations and companies have established homes across the country to fill the increasing gap between availability and numbers requiring residential care, so today we have a mixed array of provision. For the adult with an ASD, however, the success or otherwise of any residential placement or supported living arrangement will depend largely on the skills and expertise of the staff supporting them and if staff do not have knowledge and understanding of the characteristics and effects of ASDs they can make the adult's life more difficult, anxious and stressful. Training will be the key, but should come from national level to ensure all staff in all settings are fully equipped to provide appropriately for all adults with ASDs. Hopefully, following the introduction of the *National Minimum Standards: Care Homes Regulations* (DoH, 2002) this will commence as the document identifies adults with ASDs specifically and states that:

> While broad in scope, these standards acknowledge the unique and complex needs of individuals and the additional specific knowledge, skills and facilities required in order for a care home to deliver an individually tailored and comprehensive service. (ibid.: 3)

In addition, *Valuing People* (DoH, 2001b) and *Better Services for People with an Autistic Spectrum Disorder* (DoH, 2006) identified that the quality of care staff was not, overall, of a high enough standard so workforce reforms are being instigated from 2007. Issues of pay, conditions of service and status are further aspects to be addressed as the current poor pay (particularly within the private sector) results in increased turnover of staff. This affects continuity of provision which is a basic need and desire for all those with ASDs. Staff retention issues must therefore be highlighted and addressed.

Currently the Supporting People government programme, established in 2003 is working to support all vulnerable adults 'to live as independently as possible' (Internet 6). For those with disabilities the programme will offer advice, support and guidance working on total involvement of the individual in all the decision-making. All available housing options will be clarified, visits can be arranged and funding issues clarified. At the first stage of making decisions about future housing needs the adult with an ASD should identify which type of accommodation they would prefer and from then informed decisions can be made. If their choice is deemed unsuitable by the parents and/or professionals involved then sympathetic discussions should be held to ensure the individual understands all concerns. Some adults with autism may consider that they already live an independent life as they get themselves up, dressed and off to the day centre, but do not fully comprehend all the other responsibilities of daily life such as budgeting, paying bills, shopping, washing and drying clothes, cooking and cleaning. Discussions will clearly need to be handled sympathetically and again success will depend on the skills of working with adults with ASDs and ASD knowledge. Availability of ASD-specific housing options is very limited and often adults with ASDs are placed in homes for adults with learning disabilities which can pose distinct problems for them and their future. It may be that the individual requested ASD-specific housing, but if this is not available in the local area then suitable alternatives will have to be considered. Barnard et al. (2001) recommended a range of ASD-appropriate housing be established with housing and social services departments working together to make improvements to what they offer: residential care placements, clustered flats and bedsits, sheltered housing, tenancies and shared equity schemes.

Alternatively, it may be that the adult with an ASD is able to remain at home with his/her family but attendance at a day centre is deemed suitable to support development and independence. However, attendance at large groups may bring its own difficulties for many with ASDs so smaller group facilities should therefore be sought if possible. Once the housing needs have been recognised and met, whether this be home care, residential care or supported living, the realities of day-to-day life will emerge that sensitive and knowledgeable staff will need to address. These will be explored later in the chapter.

Employment

The government considers that 'employment is the route to increased social inclusion' (DoH, 2001b) and if we reflect on the current figure of 6 per cent for adults with ASDs in employment (Barnard et al., 2001) we see that opportunities are severely limited. To enable increased independence all adults who are capable of gaining and retaining employment should be supported in doing so and as professionals we should not assume those with ASDs are probably unlikely to be able to work. Our expectations should be high but achievable.

Even a voluntary position for a few hours a week can increase independence, self-confidence and therefore well-being. If the individual's characteristics are reflected upon it can be seen that routine, familiarity and limited social situations could offer an adult with an ASD successful employment. For example, routine data processing in an office would require little social interaction as engagement is mostly with the computer, regular data inputting would offer familiarity and the office day can be structured as much or as little as is needed. With the determination to make it work the support worker and prospective employer could devise systems to support the adult with the support worker acting as the link between work and home. Other possible positions would include working in kitchens with routine tasks, working in a library or a super-market (with limited interaction with the public if needed) and other office-based roles. Success or otherwise will rely strongly on the belief and commitment of the support worker who has in-depth knowledge of the adult's individual ASD difficulties and will therefore be well placed to make informed and purposeful decisions.

All the above would be more likely to happen if national strategies were implemented to encourage local authorities to develop this area of their work further. The Valuing People strategy and Better Lives for Adults with ASDs frameworks both recommend it, but strong leadership will be needed at national and local levels to instigate positive change. In addition, issues connected with reduced benefits due to earning a wage should not be such that they become a barrier to meaningful employment. Learning Disability Partnership Boards should also ensure that within their area there is a range of courses available to adults with ASDs spanning vocational and academic qualifications and courses as well as preparation-for-work courses for those embarking on seeking employment.

Access to health services

Historically adults with ASD generally fall between health departments when it comes to their initial diagnosis and assessment. In some areas of the country they could be assessed by the mental health department, in another it could be the learning disabilities department while somewhere else it could be the psychiatric department. Yet can each of the professionals involved expect to have in-depth knowledge of ASDs? The NAS (Barnard et al., 2001) called for training for all health professionals, but specifically those with diagnostic responsibilities, to improve healthcare assessments. In addition they recommended that diagnostic and assessment centres be offered in every area to improve the quality of diagnostic services and also act as a local ASD resource base which could be utilised by professionals from all agencies as well as parents and carers.

As one of the key areas of difficulty for adults with ASDs is that of communication it may also be very difficult to ascertain and assess individual health needs effectively unless the professional involved is skilled in dealing with ASDs. The Valuing People strategy also highlighted that adults with learning disabilities are less likely to undergo routine health screenings to reduce later effects of conditions such as high cholesterol, high blood pressure, diabetes, heart disease and cancer. Further the use of psychotic medication with limited positive outcomes is an area for concern. Such issues need to be addressed.

For national changes to occur the Valuing People strategy proposed that all adults with learning disability should have a Health Facilitator by 2003, a Health Action Plan in place by 2005 and inequalities relating to access to healthcare be diminished (DoH, 2001b). More specifically for adults with ASDs the DoH Better Services framework (2006) recommends that the Health Facilitator will be the key person who ensures improved access to health services for all adults with ASDs. Arguably the time when most slip through the net is at the transition stage between children's and adult's services so the professionals involved in creating the transition plan must ensure that any health needs are identified and provided for. Yet Barnard et al. (2001) reported that at transition (when only 53 per cent secured a transition plan) only 11 per cent of these involved input from relevant health professionals.

Person-centred planning and advocacy

Person-centred planning (PCP) involves putting the adult with an ASD at the centre of all discussions and including them in decisions regarding their own lives. The focus will not be on their difficulties and what they cannot do but rather be approached from the perspective of what skills and attributes they do have, and build from there. The Better Services for Adults with ASDs framework (DoH, 2006) supports the use of PCP to ensure the wishes and concerns of the individual are acknowledged and addressed within a supportive framework involving parents, family members and professionals who know the adult. In this environment it is hoped that the adult would feel safe and be able to contribute to the process to bring about the changes they want for their own life and future. The process should help to develop increased choice and independence, confidence and self-esteem and result in positive outcomes. PCP should therefore explore with the individual all aspects of their life, consider their wishes and views and devise appropriate ways forward to enable change.

Consequences of getting it wrong

All of the above are seen as key areas of concern for adults with ASDs, each requiring significant changes to promote increased rights, choice and inclusion as equal members within society. The evidence from reports clearly shows what happens if we do not get things right and the outcomes can have devastating effects on the lives of the adults themselves as well as their families. As an example, if an adult is remaining in the family home but as a result a parent cannot maintain full-time employment, then the financial impact is clearly considerable as state benefits will rarely equal paid employment remuneration.

In addition, the confidence and self-esteem of the parent may well be diminished. Engagement in accepted family activities such as going shopping and enjoying a meal out can be immensely difficult to manage if the adult's behaviour becomes unacceptable, and therefore siblings are also affected. The list is endless. So how can we as professionals aim to improve our provision within these key areas?

General strategies for use

Staff knowledge of ASDs will be the single most powerful tool professionals have but if we combine this with knowledge specific to each individual from the adults themselves and their family members we will be better informed to implement positive changes and appropriate activities. The parents will know the adult best and will have experienced most, if not all, of the behaviours that professionals will be faced with. Parental knowledge of how best to support their adult child through these difficulties can become guiding knowledge for professionals. Even though the adult may not be living at home it would be hoped that regular or occasional visits home are possible, so it is crucial that parents and professionals work together at every step of the way. Many of the individual difficulties experienced by an adult with an ASD will be relevant to professionals and parents when considering any of the aforementioned areas such as housing, health and employment. The following strategies will therefore not be restricted to any specific situation but should be considered for any situation that may arise. Examples may refer to one situation but would not automatically exclude consideration in other situations.

Professionals should appreciate the difficulties the adult may experience with too many people, too much background noise, too much visual stimulation, reading difficulties, communication difficulties, lack of ability to interpret gestures and/or facial expressions, dislike of unfamiliar environments, stereotypical behaviours and lack of imagination in any given situation. Each of these factors should be taken into account and addressed when working with an adult with an ASD.

In Chapter 4 we explored the three areas of impairment experienced by adults with ASDs: social communication, social interaction and imagination. For each area of impairment we further explored a detailed list of characteristics and behaviours that could be evident. A few basic examples were utilised in Chapter 4 to illustrate key points. Due to the individuality of ASDs we need to consider each person with an ASD separately, consider their strengths and areas of difficulty and then devise ways to tackle a specific difficulty in an informed manner. This can be done through a PCP approach which would focus on key areas of daily life that could be improved and identify specific activities that could be instigated to bring about positive change. These do not necessarily need to be major changes as sometimes support with simple tasks can make a considerable difference to someone's daily life and have a far-reaching impact on other aspects of their life. For example, enabling an adult to make his/her own hot drinks may increase independence and enhance self-confidence. As a result the adult may then feel more relaxed within the home and be able to engage with additional learning tasks.

Social communication and interaction difficulties include the lack of useful social language, lack of desire to communicate, echolalia, inability to understand the process of conversation and inability to transfer learnt communication from one situation into another. For the adult with an ASD this can lead to a range of difficulties within a world that is fundamentally social. We should also remember that adults with ASDs have considerable difficulties integrating with other people and engaging in a social context as the preferred world is likely to be one devoid of interaction with other people.

Such issues can make living in a group home or attending a day centre particularly stressful for the individual and the benefits of attending a day centre must be weighed up against the negative effects to validate continued attendance. Issues such as noise levels, visual stimuli and numbers of people nearby may all have a negative impact. If attendance is agreed upon then supporting strategies must be devised to ensure areas of anxiety are accommodated, such as a quiet space which the adult can go to whenever stress levels escalate. Once the key causes of stress and anxiety are identified, strategies should be easier to develop, particularly if the individual, the day centre staff and the key worker from the home work together. For those adults who cannot contribute verbally, alternative strategies need to be in place to enable them to participate in another form (see social communication below). Adults with ASDs may usually only display aggressive, self-harming or unacceptable social behaviours when they are experiencing increased anxiety, stress, confusion or change so professionals and parents should consider ways to identify the causal factor and create changes at that point. It would be inappropriate to attempt to eliminate the resulting behaviour as this is not, in itself, the problem.

Another significant time of potential difficulty is celebrations, whether Christmas, birthday or other significant occasions. At such times it is common to welcome additional visitors into the home (family or residential home), to have additional decorations, to have parties, presents and unusual foods, yet each of these can pose difficulties for the adult with an ASD. So Christmas festivities, which invariably contain all these elements, can be particularly stressful for the adult with an ASD. Although some adults may remove themselves from the room and therefore appear rude or react negatively, much will depend on how well the situation is managed and many adults with ASDs can learn to cope within such an environment. They may not enjoy it particularly but they can endure it. Whatever happens the rest of the family members should not be deprived of their festivities, so arguably compromise is the key. Awareness that the difficulties exist, preparing the adult for the occasion and devising strategies to support them will all help.

Adults with ASDs are also likely to have difficulties understanding the views and feelings of others so may come across as hurtful, rude or spiteful. An adult may know that a family friend or fellow resident is ill in hospital and that important people around him/her are upset as the prognosis is not positive but it may not be possible for them to verbalise their own concern or to empathise with the others. On occasions this may result in them saying something inappropriate about the situation or simply not talking about it as it is stressful to do so. Yet this could be considered as not caring. For parents of adult children, never having heard their 'child' say they love you can be very hurtful, but invariably as parental understanding of ASDs expands it becomes easier to see it does not mean they are not loved, simply that it cannot be expressed.

A further difficulty is the inability to interpret body language, gestures or facial expressions. In a room with other people we can all think of situations we have experienced in which a frown or shake of the head to someone you know can avoid them saying or doing something inappropriate. This will not necessarily be understood by the adult with an ASD but with patience some of these can be learnt through social skills and emotional development training. Many adults with ASDs may have a favourite topic on which their knowledge is immense, but they may not appreciate that others may not want to listen to them for considerable periods of time and this can result in others ignoring them and walking away or interrupting them. The adult may feel that by continuing at length they are engaging in meaningful conversation which could lead to friendships but as they do not understand the 'rules' and are unable to pick up clues from body language and facial expressions they continue with their monologue. However, from a different perspective, if the adult is aware of their own difficulties in fitting into a conversation, by monopolising the conversation they avoid the risk of getting it wrong, so it is more of a self-preservation tactic that an attempt to be rude or inconsiderate. If, as well as monopolising the conversation, the adult with ASD speaks in a very laborious, measured or monotonous tone then the difficulties could be compounded further. However, this aspect is due to an inability to appreciate the importance of pitch and intonation in speech, thus there is no need to use it.

While adults with ASDs have difficulties understanding the facial expressions of others they may also wish to avoid direct conversation through using peripheral vision as it is less confrontational. As long as others present understand this it does not need to pose problems, but when in public such behaviour may be considered as rude as it can demonstrate boredom or lack of interest in the speaker. Awareness and understanding is again the key.

One key area of difficulty is that of friendships and relationships as invariably the adult will desire to have a friend or best friend but will not understand the 'rules' of friendship. For this reason adults with ASDs become vulnerable if not supported effectively. Inappropriate approaches to strangers and/or known people, lack of understanding of touch or personal space, the desire to be liked resulting in being taking advantage of and over-possessiveness are all concerns. Once a friendship has been established the rules of maintaining that friendship will not generally be understood so again problems are likely.

The key to social difficulties is for key workers, mentors and parents to be aware of which aspects of socialising present the biggest problems for the individual. Again it is a case of identifying the causes of the difficulties and then addressing them. Group work, one-to-one work using social skills training activities and/or role play are likely to lead to some improvements, but in this area responsible professionals must remain vigilant to identify and prevent difficulties whenever possible. Professionals and parents alike would find the work of Plimley and Bowen (2007) particularly useful in developing appropriate strategies to support social skills.

With regard to *imagination and stereotypical behaviours,* we saw in Chapter 4 that difficulties such as resistance to change, repetitive body movements, unusual responses to stimuli, lack of awareness of 'normal' behaviour and/or self-harming are common. Clearly these can create particular difficulties within any environment. In public, when perhaps driving to the supermarket for the regular weekly shop, there may well be a traffic diversion taking you on a different route. For some adults with ASDs this will cause immediate confusion that can monopolise their conversation for a considerable time, with no amount of explanation seeming to help. This simple break from the familiar routine will have caused the individual confusion, uncertainty and anxiety which can be difficult to reduce or eliminate. What we need to remember is that the realities of normal life automatically result in the need to be able to accept change, as changes happen throughout life. For those adults with ASDs their life is far more difficult for them to comprehend and make sense of. By developing strategies to cope with daily life they enable themselves to participate, but when changes occur, especially unexpected changes, the anxiety, fear and confusion mount up.

Obsessional interests and/or ritualistic behaviours can also impact on the daily life of the adult with an ASD. For the adult that is obsessed with watching a particular television programme and wants everyone else in the room to be quiet while it is on, we can appreciate that difficulties and possible inappropriate behaviours are likely to become evident. The inability to understand that others are not as passionate about the programme or simply wish to see something on another channel may cause arguments to develop. Yet it may be that a television could be allowed in the adult's bedroom where the programme could be viewed without causing anyone else any difficulties. Alternatively the programme could be recorded and watched at a different time. It is the responsibility of parents and professionals to devise strategies that are sensitive to the needs of all residents and are likely to minimise potential upsets and anxiety.

Stereotypical behaviours such as rocking, hand flapping and toe walking tend to diminish from childhood as the individual matures but may still be evident or re-emerge at times of stress and anxiety. Others should therefore be sensitive to spot such occurrences and try to determine the cause of the anxiety. Identifying the cause and addressing that issue should help settle the behaviour. However, there are some adults with ASDs that show unusual behaviours when walking or travelling which clearly can create considerable difficulties, yet again if we can identify the reason for such behaviour then we can devise supportive strategies. However, for the adult with hypersensitive hearing who can hear an emergency vehicle long before anyone else, the fear of knowing how loud and painful it will become as it gets nearer can be overwhelming and result in unusual or repetitive behaviours which are difficult to alleviate. I know that if I was in a situation where I knew pain and distress was on its way, then I would use every avoidance strategy I had to remove it.

So what strategies can be implemented to support the adults we work with or care for?

- Always support an adult's poor communication skills with pictorial or written information. For example, provide a list of common items that are likely to be requested so the adult can show you the picture or list instead of relying on making themselves understood.

- Use pictures or written lists to identify the stages needed to complete common tasks such as making a cup of tea or showering and dressing.

- Use pictures or a written timetable to outline the activities for any one day to avoid uncertainties and confusion.

- Examine the causes of difficult or inappropriate behaviours and develop ways in which to enable the adult to cope more appropriately. For example, teach alternative behaviours such as leaving a room if someone is upsetting them, or going to a quiet space if feeling anxious.

- Understand the impact of sensory difficulties as this can impact on a range of issues such as eating, the volume of the television or other people and shopping.

- Use social skills training to support development and understanding of the social world.

- Develop skills to cope with unexpected changes. For example, always carry an umbrella in case of rain and discuss that change is not always negative.

- Develop awareness that some behaviours are unacceptable to others and as such could be kept private. For example, if you are distressed in the supermarket you use other developed strategies to cope until you are back in the car or at home.

- Develop the skill of 'asking' for help when feeling anxious or stressed either by telling the key worker or, if non-verbal, developing a sign or using a picture to convey the message.

- Work on communication skills, including the understanding of the rules of conversation.

- Develop obsessions in a more controlled, manageable or advantageous manner, such as playing on computer games to help develop social interaction and communication skills.

- Teach relaxation skills or alternative skills to overcome difficult situations, such as counting to ten or focusing on a pleasurable situation.

The following case studies will hopefully demonstrate how, from an initial PCP review, targets can be identified for future weeks or months. One target can then be further broken down to recognise the steps needed to achieve the desired outcome. The first case study considers Stephen and his desire to secure employment which was expressed at his PCP discussion. The first stage was to prepare him for job applications and interviews. After a few months he did manage to secure a position so the revised target was to ensure he could manage the job on a daily basis and maintain it. His strengths and areas of potential difficulty, with the strategies to address these, are outlined.

Case study 8.1 Stephen

Stephen's strengths

- Computer literate.
- Logical and mathematical brain.
- Desires employment within this field.
- Competent at using most standard computer applications and wishes to work with numbers.
- Keen to learn more about computers and computer applications.
- Competent reading skills.
- Accommodating if employer would like to phase in the job.
- Would not disturb others by engaging in conversation unnecessarily.
- Can work flexible hours.
- Applies himself well to set tasks.
- Reliable and punctual.
- Hard-working.
- Eager to please.

Stephen's areas of potential difficulty

- Support would be needed in Stephen's care home to ensure he had all the materials needed every day and was ready on time and to discuss work related issues with him.
- Does not like too much noise.

- Prefers to work in isolation from others.
- Requires a clear, explicit checklist of jobs to do to remain on task.
- May appear abrupt in manner due to lack of social skills.
- May appear inappropriate in social situations by monopolising conversations.
- May need strategies to support him if he is unsure about something.
- Would need a colleague to monitor his work progress.
- Would need preparation for unexpected changes (e.g. fire alarm, colleague not attending work).
- Could be a target for verbal abuse due to his unusual behaviours and other difficulties.

Strategies and responsibilities to be deployed

- Stephen's key worker in the care home would meet initially with Stephen and an employee of the company to discuss the position in depth, plan appropriate strategies, share knowledge and establish a system of regular meetings.
- The designated employee will become Stephen's mentor in the workplace and would hold the key worker's phone number for unexpected situations.
- Stephen's desk area to be screened off from the rest of the office and facing a wall to minimise distractions.
- Stephen's key worker to attend a staff meeting at the place of work to explain ASDs and Stephen's specific areas of difficulty and unusual behaviours.
- Stephen's mentor and key worker to devise a list of appropriate behaviours in the workplace to be displayed by Stephen's desk.
- Stephen be allowed to take his breaks in an identified quiet space.
- The quiet space was designated for Stephen's use if he was feeling stressed or anxious.
- A list of Stephen's tasks for the day to be placed on his desk before he arrives each day. At regular intervals Stephen's mentor would ensure he was completing tasks satisfactorily and remaining on task.
- Stephen would have monthly meetings with his mentor and key worker to discuss progress and work for the next month. Training opportunities could also be discussed at these meetings.
- Stephen's key worker to provide him with a list of things to pack in his bag each morning – initially he/she will check this is done, but over time it would be hoped he would develop independence with this task.
- Stephen's key worker and mentor would develop strategies to teach Stephen to use if he was unsure, had a query, ran out of work, needed to use the cloakroom or needed some time out due to distress and anxiety.

Clearly these strategies are individual to Stephen but it can be seen that with commitment on the part of the key worker and the employer it would not be too difficult to adapt them to suit many other adults with an ASD. If reading is not a developed skill then lists and instructions can be displayed pictorially. Success is likely to follow and employers have registered their pleasure at having staff members with ASDs due to their loyalty, reliability and work ethic, often not equalled by the rest of the workforce (Howlin, 2004). This is not to suggest, however, that problems cannot arise, but with understanding from the mentor and key worker these can each be explored and addressed as they emerge. There will also be some adults with ASDs that do not possess adequate skills to secure paid employment due to the severity of their difficulties, yet this should not mean that their lives should remain unfulfilled. The challenge is to identify the strengths and weaknesses of each and every adult and devise appropriate ways forward to develop their existing skills further in a planned way which improves their quality of life and enhances their skill range.

The second case study considers Lucy who has very limited useful language and uses her language mostly in an echolalic manner. It has been identified by the staff in the care home that when asked if she wants a cup of tea, she repeats the sentence back, which is interpreted as her agreement and she is given a cup of tea. Over time, however, she has been either leaving the tea or becoming very anxious when it arrives and resorting to rocking and biting her arm. The staff decided it would be appropriate for her to develop the skill to choose and make her own drink, so a plan was devised to offer Lucy greater control over her choice of drinks as well as teach her a new skill. As Lucy responded well and worked well with her key worker it was agreed that her key worker Sarah would develop this with Lucy.

Case study 8.2 Lucy

Lucy's strengths

- Lucy likes Sarah, her key worker, and always tries to please her.
- Despite her poor language skills Lucy responds well to pictorial representation.
- Lucy follows instructions well.
- Lucy is careful when in the kitchen and follows the safety rules. She already helps at meal times with some basic food preparation.
- Lucy is patient when working with Sarah and listens well.
- Lucy is persistent if she wants to achieve something.

Areas of potential difficulty

- Safety issues.

- Ensuring quiet time to allow Sarah and Lucy to work uninterrupted while developing the skill. This was organised between the staff.

- Timetabling regular slots for the 'teaching' of the skill ensuring cover is sufficient.

Strategies used

- Sarah took photos of a pack of tea bags, a jar of coffee and a tub of hot chocolate. These were laminated for durability. Thumbnail versions were also printed and laminated.

- Sarah spent time working with Lucy playing with the new cards – matching the cards to the correct jars out of a selection of assorted tins, jars and packs. This was to familiarise Lucy with registering the card to the real object.

- Sarah used the cards to demonstrate to Lucy that by handing over one of the cards to a member of staff she would be given the matching drink.

- Sarah then used this strategy for a week.

- A similar set of cards was produced with the addition of a kettle next to the packet or jar. This was to indicate that Lucy wanted to make her own drink.

- On the reverse of these cards were pictures of the materials needed for the task.

- Sarah worked with Lucy in the kitchen when no others were present and ensured that the worktop was clear, apart from the kettle, to avoid any possible confusion.

- Sarah showed Lucy how to find the materials in the same order they were shown on the back of the card. This worked from left to right: cup – tea bag – spoon – sugar – kettle – milk.

- Sarah worked through the process with Lucy and they both enjoyed their drinks together.

- Over time Sarah showed Lucy that if she gave the card without the kettle on it to a member of staff they would make her a drink, but if she used the other card they would take her into the kitchen and help her to make it herself.

- Lucy was given a set of the smaller version thumbnail cards on a clip she attached to her belt so they were always accessible.

A simple process spaced over a period of two months moved Lucy from a dependent young lady who was often frustrated by other people's decisions and her inability to communicate effectively to a more independent young lady with improved confidence. Although it may seem a minor achievement, for this young lady it was a major accomplishment. Through identifying the potential problems and developing new skills in a carefully planned and structured way Lucy's life in the home was considerably improved.

This basic process can be repeated to address a range of issues for adults with ASDs:

1 Identify the behaviour you wish to work on or the skill you wish to develop.
2 For behaviours, examine the causal factors or triggers and see if changes can be made to these.
3 Identify one clear target to work towards.
4 List the adult's skills and areas of difficulty related to this target.
5 List the steps which need to be taken to achieve the target.
6 Identify any allied issues that need to be clarified or sorted (such as staffing and the quiet time in Lucy's case study).
7 Identify the person responsible for working on the target and any materials needed.
8 Set a realistic timescale and review date.
9 Ensure the process is logged in records.

Staffing issues

Notably within the area of private residential care it is common practice for care workers to be low paid and often staff have no or limited qualifications and training in the field of work. Due to the low pay and thus low status of the work the turnover in staff is often significant. Those who secure jobs in the field and are successful in what they do generally have an intuitive ability to work with adults with ASDs, who at times can be very demanding, frustrating and challenging. Such employees should be nurtured and highly valued by their employers as they could invariably secure more lucrative employment elsewhere and in a different sector of work but prefer to stay in the position which gives them great personal satisfaction. Training opportunities should be made available to them to support their own professional development. However, the increased turnover of staff is a contributing factor to the difficulties experienced by the residents with ASDs within homes, as generally change means anxiety, uncertainty and sometimes fear. In Lucy's case study, for example, if the key worker Sarah were to have left before the target was met Lucy could have refused to work with anyone else or progress towards the target itself could simply have stopped. Alternatively Lucy may not have got on so well with her replacement key worker so the chances of success were reduced. Any of these would be likely to have a significant impact on Lucy and her well-being. Therefore the workforce reforms proposed by the government are to be welcomed.

Summary

With thought, determination and adequate knowledge and skills many adults with ASDs can experience improvements in a variety of aspects of their lives. Knowledge, flexibility and commitment can enable strategies to be devised to reduce stress and anxiety and introduce new skills, from making a cup of tea to securing and maintaining employment. From the PCP, areas for improvement can be identified and realistic targets set for both the short and long term. These can then be broken down into manageable steps to ensure success.

Whatever field of caring work a professional is engaged in they can inform others of useful strategies or be the key worker that actually implements those strategies. Within the philosophy of Valuing People, improvements can be made and greater choice and independence be granted to the vulnerable adults we work with or care for.

Key issues

❖ Professionals' knowledge and understanding of ASDs and the individuals we work with will support our planning and the selection of approaches to be used.

❖ Periods of transition will require thorough planning and appropriate support for the individual.

❖ The individual's views must be taken into account.

❖ Barriers to improvements must be identified and addressed.

Suggestions for discussion (professionals)

1. Assess the ASD training needs of the staff through questionnaires to the staff (teaching and non-teaching), the parents of students with ASDs and the students themselves asking their views.

2. Act upon the findings.

3. Ensure all members of staff have knowledge of appropriate strategies to implement and have the means do so.

Suggestions for discussion (parents)

1. Ensure the accommodation your adult child is living in is aware of any strategies that you have employed successfully at home that could be adopted in the setting.

2. Ask to be involved in regular meetings relating to the planning for your family member.

3. Ensure the staff know the specific strengths and difficulties of your family member.

4. Ensure appropriate opportunities are available to help your family member achieve their full potential.

Suggested further reading

Howlin, P. (2004) *Autism and Asperger Syndrome: Preparing for Adulthood.* 2nd Edition. London: Routledge.

Plimley, L. and Bowen, M. (2007) *Autistic Specturm Disorders in the Secondary School.* London: Paul Chapman.

Bibliography

Anderson-Ford, D. (1994) Legal aid: how special education is defined in law, in S. Sandow (ed.), *Whose Special Need?* London: Paul Chapman Publishing.

Atkinson, D. (2005) Narratives and people with learning disabilities, in Grant, G., Goward, P., Richardson, M. and Ramcharan, P. (eds) (2005) *Learning Disability. A Life Cycle Approach to Valuing People*. Maidenhead: Open University Press.

Audit Commission (1986) *Making a Reality of Community Care*. London: Audit Commission.

Audit Commission (2002). *Special Educational Needs: A Mainstream Issue*. London: Audit Commission.

Baird, G. (2006) in Fleming, N., Autism in children '10 times higher' than first thought. *Daily Telegraph*, 15 July.

Barnard, J, Prior. A. and Potter, D. (2000) *Inclusion and Autism: Is it Working?* London: NAS.

Barnard, J., Broach, S., Potter, D. and Prior, A. (2002) *Autism in Schools: Crisis or Challenge?* London: NAS.

Barnard, J., Harvey, V., Potter, D. and Prior, A. (2001) *Ignored or Ineligible? The Reality for Adults with Autism Spectrum Disorders*. London: NAS.

Batten, A., Corbett, C., Rosenblatt, M., Withers, L. and Yuille, R. (2006) *Make School Make Sense. Autism and Education: The Reality for Families Today*. London: NAS.

Baworowski, L. (2002) Long climb to the day centre. *Communication*, Spring.

Bigby, C. (2005) Growing Old: Adapting to change and realizing a sense of belonging, continuity and purpose, in Grant, G., Goward, P., Richardson, M. and Ramcharan, P. (eds) *Learning Disability. A Life Cycle Approach to Valuing People*. Maidenhead: Open University Press.

Brammer, A. (2005) Learning disability and the law, in Grant, G., Goward, P., Richardson, M. and Ramcharan, P. (eds) *Learning Disability. A Life Cycle Approach to Valuing People*. Maidenhead: Open University Press.

Breakey, C. (2006) *The Autism Spectrum and Further Education: A Guide to Good Practice.* London: Jessica Kingsley.

Broach, S., Camgöz, Ş., Heather, C., Owen, G., Potter, D. and Prior, A. (2003) *Autism: Rights in Reality.* London: NAS.

Carpenter, B. (1997) *Families in Context.* London: David Fulton.

Clark, J. (2003) *Independence Matters: An Overview of the Performance of Social Care Services for Physically and Sensory Disabled People.* London: SSI/DoH.

Cope, C. (2003) *Fulfilling Lives: Inspection of Social Care Services for People with Learning Disabilities.* London: DoH.

Court, S.D.M. (1976) *Fit for the Future: The Report of the Committee on Child Health Services. Volume 1* (Court Report). London: HMSO.

Davis, B. (2001) *Breaking Autism's Barrier: A Father's Story.* London: Jessica Kingsley.

DES (1970) *Education (Handicapped Children) Act.* London: HMSO.

DES (1978) *The Report of the Committee of Enquiry into the Education of Handicapped Children and Young People* (Warnock Report). London: HMSO.

DES (1981) *Education Act.* London: HMSO.

DfEE (1993) *Education Act.* London: HMSO.

DfEE (1994) *Code of Practice on the Identification and Assessment of Special Educational Needs.* London: HMSO.

DfEE (1996) *Nursery Education and Grant Maintained Schools Act.* London: HMSO.

DfEE (1997) *Excellence for All Children: Meeting Special Educational Needs.* London: HMSO.

DfES (2001a) *Special Educational Needs and Disability Discrimination Act.* Nottingham: DfES.

DfES (2001b) *Special Educational Needs Code of Practice.* Nottingham: DfES.

DfES (2001c) *Inclusive Schooling: Children with Special Educational Needs.* Nottingham: DfES.

DfES (2001d) *Special Educational Needs Toolkit.* Nottingham: DfES.

DfES (2002a) *Education Act.* Nottingham: DfES.

DfES (2002b) *Autistic Spectrum Disorders: Good Practice Guidance.* Nottingham: DfES.

DfES (2003) *Every Child Matters* Nottingham: DfES.

DfES (2004a) *Every Child Matters: Next Steps.* Nottingham: DfES.

DfES (2004b) *Children Act.* London: HMSO.

DfES (2004c) *Removing Barriers to Achievement: The Government's Strategy for SEN.* Nottingham: DfES.

DfES (2005a) *Education Act.* Nottingham: DfES.

DfES (2005b) *14–19 Education and Skills White Paper.* Nottingham: DfES.

DfES (2006) *Youth Matters: Next Steps.* Nottingham: DfES.

DfES/DoH (2002) *Autistic Spectrum Disorders: Good Practice Guidance.* London: DfES.

DHSS (1971) *Better Services for the Mentally Handicapped.* London: HMSO.

Disability Rights Task Force (1999) *From Exclusion to Inclusion: A Report of the Disability Rights Task Force on Civil Rights for Disabled People.* London: DRTF.

DoH (1983) *Mental Health Act.* London: HMSO.

DoH (1988) *Community Care: Agenda for Action.* London: HMSO.

DoH (1989) *Caring for People.* London: HMSO.

DoH (1990) *National Health Services and Community Care Act.* London: HMSO.

DoH (1991) *The Children Act Guidance and Regulations. Volume 2: Family Support, Daycare and Educational Provision for Young Children.* London: HMSO.

DoH (1998) *A First Class Service: Quality in the New NHS.* Leeds: DoH.

DoH (2000a) *Care Standards Act.* London: Stationery Office.

DoH (2000b) *The NHS Plan.* London: Stationery Office.

DoH (2001a) *The Health and Social Care Act.* London: Stationery Office.

DoH (2001b) *Valuing People: A New Strategy for Learning Disability in the 21st Century.* London: Stationery Office.

DoH (2002) *Care Homes for Younger Adults and Adult Placements: National Minimum Standards – Care Home Regulations.* London: Stationery Office.

DoH (2004a) *National Service Framework for Children, Young People and Maternity Services.* London: Stationery Office.

DoH (2004b) *A Parent's Guide to Direct Payments.* London: DoH.

DoH (2004c) *National Standards. Local Action: Health and Social Care Standards and Planning Framework.* London: Stationery Office.

DoH (2004d) *Agenda for Change.* London: Stationery Office.

DoH (2005) *Mental Capacity Act.* London: Stationery Office.

DoH (2006) *Better Services for People with Autistic Spectrum Disorders.* London: Stationery Office.

DWP (2006) *Improving Work Opportunities for People with a Learning Disability.* London: DWP.

Florian, L. (2007) *The Sage Handbook of Special Education.* London: Sage.

Frith, U. (1991) *Autism and Asperger Syndrome.* Cambridge: Cambridge University Press.

Gillingham, G. (1995) *Autism: Handle With Care.* Arlington, Texas: Future Horizons.

Grandin, T. (1995) *Thinking in Pictures and Other Reports from My Life with Autism.* New York: Vintage.

Grant, G., Goward, P., Richardson, M. and Ramcharan, P. (eds) (2005) *Learning Disability. A Life Cycle Approach to Valuing People.* Maidenhead: Open University Press.

Greig, R. (2006) *Values and Visions: Services for People with a Learning Disability.* London: Valuing People Support Team.

Hanbury, M. (2005) *Educating Children with Autistic Spectrum Disorders.* London: Paul Chapman.

Harker, M. and King, N. (2004) *Tomorrow's Big Problem: Housing Options for People with Autism.* London: NAS.

Her Majesty's Government (2005a) *Youth Matters.* London: Stationery Office.

Her Majesty's Government (2005b) *The Government's Annual Report on Learning Disability. Valuing People: Making Things Better.* London: Stationery Office.

Her Majesty's Government (2006) *Introducing the Office for Disability Issues.* London: Stationery Office.

HMSO (1995) *Disability Discrimination Act 1995.* London: Stationery Office.

HMSO (1998) *Human Rights Act 1998.* London: Stationery Office.

HMSO (2005) *Disability Discrimination Act 2005.* London: Stationery Office.

House of Commons (2006) *Special Educational Needs: Third Report of Sessions 2005–6, Volume One.* London: Stationery Office.

Howlin, P. (2004) *Autism and Aspergers Syndrome: Preparing for Adulthood.* (2nd edition). London: Routledge.

Jones, G., Jordan, R., and Morgan, H. (2001) *All about Autistic Spectrum Disorders.* London: Mental Health Foundation.

Jones, L. J. C. (2000) Reshaping Welfare: Voices from the debate, in Davies C., Finlay, L. and Bullman, A. (eds) *Changing Practice in Health and Social Care.* London: The Open University & Sage.

Jones, L. and Tucker, S. (2000) Exploring continuity and change, in Brechin, A., Brown, and Eby, M. A. (eds) *Critical Practice in Health and Social Care.* London: The Open University & Sage.

Jordan, R. (1999) *Autistic Spectrum Disorders: An Introductory Handbook for Practitioners.* London: David Fulton.

Kanner, L. (1943) Autistic disturbances of affective contact. *Nervous Child.* 2, 217–250.

Knapp, M. and Jarbrink, K. (2001) The economic impact of autism in Britain. *Autism.* 5, 1, 7–21.

Lawson, W. (2000) *Life Behind Glass: A Personal Account of Autistic Spectrum Disorder.* London: Jessica Kingsley.

Lawson, W. (2002) *Understanding and Working with the Spectrum of Autism – An Insider's View.* London: Jessica Kingsley.

Learning Disability Taskforce (2004) *Rights, Independence, Choice and Inclusion.* London: Learning Disability Taskforce.

Lindsay, G. (1997) Values and legislation, in Lindsay G. and Thompson D. (eds), *Values into Practice in Special Education.* London: David Fulton.

Loynes, F. (2001a) *The Impact of Autism: A Report Compiled for the All Party Parliamentary Group on Autism.* London: APPGA.

Loynes, F. (2001b) *The Rising Challenge: A Survey of Local Authorities on Educational Provision for Pupils with Autistic Spectrum Disorders.* London: APPGA.

McClimens, A. (2005) From vagabonds to Victorian values, in Grant, G., Goward. P., Richardson, M. and Ramcharan, P. (eds) *Learning Disability: A Life Cycle Approach to Valuing People.* Maidenhead: Open University Press.

Mesibov, G. and Howley, M. (2003) *Accessing the Curriculum for Pupils with Autistic Spectrum Disroders.* London: David Fulton.

Ministry of Education (1944) *Education Act.* London: HMSO.

Moore, C. (2004) *George and Sam.* London: Penguin.

Morgan, H. (1998 *Adults with Autism: A Guide to Theory and Practice.* Cambridge: Cambridge University Press.

National Autistic Society (1999) *Opening the Door. A Report on Diagnosis and Assessment of Autism and Asperger Syndrome Based on Personal Experiences.* London: National Autistic Society.

National Autistic Society (2001) *Approaches to Autism.* London: National Autistic Society.

National Autistic Society (2002) *Taking Responsibility: Good Practice Guidelines for Services – Adults with Asperger Syndrome.* London: National Autistic Society.

National Autistic Society (2004) *A Place in Society.* London: National Autistic Society.

Ofsted (2004) *Special Educational Needs and Disability: Towards Inclusive Schools.* London: Ofsted.

Ofsted (2005) *Framework for the Inspection of Schools.* London: Ofsted.

Peacock, G., Forest, A. and Mills, R. (1996) *Autism – The Invisible Children.* London: NAS.

Peeters, T. (1997) *Autism: From Theoretical Understanding to Educational Intervention.* London: Whurr.

Plimley, L. and Bowen, M. (2006) *Autistic Spectrum Disorders in the Secondary School.* London: Paul Chapman.

Plimley, L. and Bowen, M. (2007) *Social Skills and Autistic Spectrum Disorders.* London: Paul Chapman.

Powell, A. (2002) *Taking Responsibility: Good Practice Guidelines for Services – Adults with Asperger Syndrome.* London: NAS.

Presland, J. (1993) Behavioural approaches, in Charlton, T. and David, K. *Managing Misbehaviour in Schools.* London: Routledge.

Ramjhun, A. F. (2002) *Implementing the Code of Practice for Children with Special Educational Needs: A Practical Guide.* London: David Fulton.

Richardson, M. (2005) Critiques of segregation and eugenics, in Grant, G., Goward, P., Richardson, M. and Ramcharan, P. (eds) *Learning Disability. A Life Cycle Approach to Valuing People.* Maidenhead: Open University Press.

Roberts, G. (1999) Supportive frameworks. *Autism.* Autumn.

Siegel, B. (1996) *The World of the Autistic Child: Understanding and Treating Autistic Spectrum Disorders.* Oxford: Oxford University Press.

SKILL (2004) *Into Higher Education 2004: The Higher Education Guide for People with Disabilities.* London: SKILL.

Styring, L. and Grant, G. (2005) Maintaining a commitment to quality, in Grant, G., Goward, P., Richardson, M. and Ramcharan, P. (eds) *Learning Disability. A Life Cycle Approach to Valuing People.* Maidenhead: Open University Press.

Talbot-Smith, A. and Pollock, A. M. (2006) *The New NHS. A Guide.* London: Routledge.

UNESCO (1994) *Salamanca Statement on Principles, Policy and Practice in Special Needs Education.* Paris: UNESCO.

United Nations (1971) *United Nations Declaration on the Rights of Mentally Retarded People.* New York: United Nations.

Wall, K. (2003) *Special Needs and Early Years: A Practitioner's Guide*. London: Paul Chapman.

Wall, K. (2004) *Autism and Early Years Practice*. London: Paul Chapman.

Wall, K. (2006) *Special Needs and Early Years: A Practitioner's Guide*. 2nd edition. London: Paul Chapman.

Waterhouse, C. and NAS Advocacy for Education team (2006) *Special Educational Needs: A Guide for Parents and Carers of Children with Autistic Spectrum Disorders*. London: NAS.

Whitaker, P. (2001) in Plimley, L. and Bowen, M. (2006) *Autistic Spectrum Disorders in the Secondary School*. London: Paul Chapman.

Whitman, T. L. (2004) The Development of Autism: A Self-regulatory Perspective. London: Jessica Kingsley.

Williams, D. (1992) *Nobody, Nowhere*. New York: Time Books.

Williams, D. (1996) *Autism: An Inside-Out Approach*. London: Jessica Kingsley.

Williams, D. (1998a) *Nobody Nowhere*. London: Jessica Kingsley.

Williams, D. (1998b) *Somebody Somewhere*. London: Jessica Kingsley.

Wiltshire, S. (1991) *Floating Cities*. London: Summit Books.

Wing, L. (ed) (1976) *Early Childhood Autism*. 2nd edition. Oxford: Pergamon Press.

Wing, L. (1991) The Relationships between Asperger's Syndrome and Kanner's Autism, in Frith, U. (ed) *Autism and Asperger's Syndrome*. Cambridge: Cambridge University Press.

Wing, L. and Gould, J (1978) Systematic recording of behaviours and skills of retarded and psychotic children, *Journal of Autism and Childhood Schizophrenia*, 8, 79–97.

World Health Organisation (1992) *ICD-10 International Statistical Classification of Diseases and Related Health Problems*. 10th edition. Geneva: WHO.

Internet references

Internet 1:   www.nas.org.uk (Accessed 21.02.2006)

Internet 2:   www teachernet.gov.uk/management/atoz/national curriculum/(Accessed 05.03.2006)

Internet 3:   www.connexions-direct.com (Accessed 01.03.2006)

Internet 4:   www.nhshistory.net/short_history.htm (Accessed 13.04.2006)

Internet 5:   www.everychildmatters.co.uk (Accessed 20.03.2005)

Internet 6:   www.direct.gov.uk/DisabledPeople/HomeAndHousing Options (Accessed 03.03.2006 and 23/07/06)

Internet 7:   www.dh.gov.uk/PolicyandGuidance/HealthandSocialCare Topics/SocialCare (Accessed 26.12.2006)

Internet 8:   www.gscc.org.uk/codes_practice.htm (Accessed 05.07.04)

Internet 9:   www.cabinetoffice.gov.uk/strategy/downloads/work_areas/
               disability/disability_report/pdf/disability.pdf (Accessed 05.11.06)
Internet 10:   www.dwp.gov.uk/asd (Accessed 24.12.06)
Internet 11:   www,dh.gov.uk/PolicyandGuidance/HealthandSocialCare
               Topics (Accessed 26.12.06)
Internet 12:   www.drc-gb.org (Accessed 15.12.06)
Internet 13:   www.nhshistory.net/primarycare (Accessed 23.07.06)
Internet 14:   www.officefordisability.gov.uk/national (Accessed 05.11.06)
Internet 15:   http://www.visionaustralia.org.au/info.aspx?page=861
Internet 16:   www.edcm.org.uk (Accessed 20.01.07)
Internet 17:   www.nadp-uk.org/membership/institutional.php
               (Accessed 19.12.06)
Internet 18:   www.TheGrayCentre.org (Accessed 06.01.07)
Internet 19:   http://www.dh.gov.uk/PublicationsAndStatistics/Publications/
               PublicationsPolicyAndGuidance/PublicationsPolicyAnd
               GuidanceArticle (Accessed 16.12.06)

Index